# POEMS

Born in Ireland in 1898, C. S. Lewis was educated at Malvern College for a year and then privately. He gained a Triple First at Oxford and was a Fellow and Tutor at Magdalen College 1925–54. In 1954 he became Professor of Medieval and Renaissance Literature at Cambridge. He was an outstanding and popular lecturer and had a deep and lasting influence on his pupils.

C. S. Lewis was for many years an atheist, and described his conversion in *Surprised by Joy*: 'In the Trinity Term of 1929 I gave in, and admitted that God was God . . . perhaps the most dejected and reluctant convert in all England.' It was this experience that helped him to understand not only apathy but active unwillingness to accept religion and, as a Christian writer, gifted with an exceptionally brilliant and logical mind and a lucid, lively style, he was without peer. He also wrote books for children, and some science fiction, besides many works of literary criticism. He died on 22 November, 1963, at his home in Oxford.

Walter Hooper was secretary to C. S. Lewis and is now the literary advisor to his estate. He lives in Oxford.

# THE
# COLLECTED POEMS
# OF C. S. LEWIS

Edited by
WALTER HOOPER

**Fount Paperbacks**
*An Imprint of HarperCollinsPublishers*

Fount Paperbacks is an imprint of
HarperCollins*Religious*,
Part of HarperCollins Publishers,
77–85 Fulham Palace Road
Hammersmith, London W6 8JB

First published in Great Britain
in 1994 by Fount Paperbacks

1 3 5 7 9 10 8 6 4 2

Introduction and Introductory Letter by C. S. Lewis
© C. S. Lewis Pte Ltd 1994
POEMS
Poems and Preface © C. S. Lewis Pte Ltd 1964
Poems from Punch as listed in the appendix
© Bradbury, Agnew & Co Ltd 1946–1954
SPIRITS IN BONDAGE Copyright C. S. Lewis 1919
A MISCELLANY OF ADDITIONAL POEMS
© C. S. Lewis Pte Ltd 1986, 1994

Walter Hooper asserts the moral right to be
identified as the editor of this work

A catalogue record for this book is
available from the British Library

ISBN 0 00 627833-7

Printed and bound in Great Britain by
HarperCollinsManufacturing, Glasgow

To
Owen Barfield

# CONTENTS

# INTRODUCTION

This volume brings together for the first time all C. S. Lewis's short poems into a single volume. It contains the two collections, *Poems* (1964) and *Spirits in Bondage: A Cycle of Lyrics* (1919) as well as a 'Miscellany' of seventeen short poems previously either unpublished or uncollected. The poems cover the whole of Lewis's life, from those he wrote as a young man of sixteen to those written within a few weeks of his death.

In planning the present volume I was fortunate in being able to consult Lewis's friend, Owen Barfield. Mr Barfield had been discussing Lewis's poems with him since they met in 1919, and he had given me much helpful advice when I was editing the *Poems* thirty years ago. He felt that both *Poems* and *Spirits in Bondage* must be regarded as 'historical documents', which should not be altered. I have, accordingly, left both those volumes intact, including my original Preface to *Poems*, and it remains to mention the new poems and how they fit into this volume.

Something must first be said about *Spirits in Bondage* which was published in 1919 when Lewis was twenty and which will be new to most readers. Except for a paperback published in the United States in 1983, the poems have been out of print in this country for over seventy-five years. The poems go back to 19 September 1914 when C. S. Lewis went to be crammed for Oxford by his father's old headmaster at Lurgan College in County Armagh. This was William T. Kirkpatrick who was living in semi-retirement in Great Bookham, Surrey. Those familiar with Lewis's autobiography, *Surprised by Joy*, will recall that he was, unbeknown to his family, an atheist when he joined Mr Kirkpatrick. One result of working with this 'purely logical entity' (ch. ix), who had left Christianity years before for rationalism, was that Lewis soon found 'the two hemi-spheres' of his mind in the sharpest contrast'. 'On the one side a many-islanded sea of poetry and myth; on the other a glib and shallow "rationalism"' (ch. xi). This is not to say that the young Lewis did not relish the dialectical rough and tumble of Kirkpatrick's methods. 'If I could please myself,' he said in *Surprised by Joy*, 'I would always live as I lived there' (ch. ix).

Nevertheless, when he arrived in Belfast during Easter 1915 for his first holiday he turned to his great love, verse, and devoted nearly all his hours to the craft of poetry and its wide variety of metrical forms. During his weeks at home he wrote several romantic lyrics. One was published in *Spirits of Bondage*. In another, 'The Hills of Down', which has remained unpublished all these years, he expressed his love for

> the green hills of Down.
> The soft low hills of Down.

From this time onwards until he went up to Oxford in 1917, Lewis spent much of every holiday writing verse. Fifty-two of the poems written during this two-year period were copied into a notebook bearing the title 'The Metrical Meditations of a Cod', 'Cod' being an Ulster expression of 'humorous and insincere self-depreciation' ('Amn't I the quare oul' cod to be doin' so and so').[1]

When Lewis arrived at University College, Oxford, on 26 April 1917, he knew he would soon be in the war and he had left his 'Metrical Medications' in the safekeeping of his Belfast friend, Arthur Greeves. Most of the colleges were being used as hospitals or for billeting cadets, and there were only eight or nine students left in University College. Lewis joined the Officers' Training Corps, but as their military duties were light at the time, he turned once again to poetry. The poems he wrote during the next few months in Oxford were copied into a notebook he and Arthur were later to refer to as the 'reddy-brown MS book containing "Lullaby" and several other poems'.

On 7 June Lewis joined a cadet battalion and moved into Keble College. 'I am in a strangely productive mood,' he wrote to Arthur

1. The unpublished 'Lewis Papers: Memoirs of the Lewis Family 1850–1930', vol. IV, p. 306.

on 10 June, 'and spend my few moments of spare time in scribbling verse ... I propose to get together all the stuff I have perpetrated and see if any kind publisher would like to take it. After that, if the fates decide to kill me at the front, I shall enjoy a 9-days immortality while friends who know nothing about poetry imagine that I must have been a genius.'[2] There was not enough time for this.

After a scarce three months' training, Lewis went to France as a 2nd Lieutenant in the Somerset Light Infantry. He arrived at the front lines on his nineteenth birthday, 29 November 1917. In December the 1st Somerset Light Infantry was located near Monchy Le-Preux, and it was while opposing guns sounded round them that Lewis probably composed his 'French Nocturne (Monchy-Le-Preux)'. One stanza of that poem is sufficient to illustrate how the voice of the poet has changed:

> What call have I to dream of anything?
> I am a wolf. Back to the world again,
> And speech of fellow-brutes that once were men
> Our throats can bark for slaughter: cannot sing.

The battalion spent Christmas and New Year under heavy enemy fire at Woringham. It was almost certainly here that Lewis began writing his 'Apology' and the 'Ode for a New Year's Day'. In the first he explains to the goddess, Despoina, why he cannot 'build a heaven of dreams in real hell'. The dejection in his 'Ode for a New Year's Day' is even grater than that of the 'Apology' because Lewis now sees that the evil God who allows all this destruction is not the same as the 'Good'. In fact, 'Good' itself is only a 'phantom' created by 'our own hearts'.

Lewis was seriously wounded in the Battle of Arras on 15 April 1918. Later, in a hospital in Etaples, he returned to poetry and quite a new interest for him – Philosophy. He was very impressed by John Locke's *Essay Concerning Human Understanding*, in which the author insists that pure reality cannot be grasped by the human mind, that substance is 'an uncertain supposition of we know not what'.

2. *They Stand Together: The Letters of C. S. Lewis to Arthur Greeves* 1914–1963 (1979), p. 192.

During his years with Mr Kirkpatrick, Lewis had mainly ignored God. Now, with nearly all his army friends either killed or missing, his outlook was changing. 'You'll be surprised to hear that my views at present are getting almost monastic about the lusts of the flesh', he wrote to Arthur on 23 May. 'They seem to me to extend the domination of matter over us: and out here where I see spirit continually dodging matter (shells, bullets, animal fears, animal pains) I have formulated my equation Matter = Nature = Satan. And on the other side Beauty, the only spiritual & non-natural thing I have yet found.'[3] Later that month Lewis was moved to Endsleigh Palace Hospital in London. On 3 June he asked Arthur to send him the 'reddy-brown MS book' because 'I have decided to copy out all my work . . . as a step towards possible publishing.' 'I believe in no God,' he reminded him, 'but I do believe that I have in me a spirit, a chip, shall we say, of universal spirit; and that, since all good & joyful things are spiritual & non-material, I must be careful not to let matter . . . get too great hold on me, & dull the one spark I have.'[4] At the end of June Lewis was moved to Ashton Court, near Bristol, where he was to be for nearly four months. It was here that his collection of poems took shape. It was sent to William Heinemann in London who said he was 'pleased to be its publisher'. In a letter to Arthur Greeves of 12 September 1918 Lewis said that his volume of poems, *Spirits in Bondage: A Cycle of Lyrics*, was 'mainly strung round the idea . . . that nature is wholly diabolical & malevolent and that God, if he exists, is outside of and in opposition to the cosmic arrangement'.[5]

Mr Heinemann and his General Manager, Charles Sheldon Evans, told Lewis that they never expected to make a commercial success out of poetry, but published it 'simply because it's good'. They asked him to make a number of small alterations in his poems as well as send substitutes for those they thought not on a level with the poet's 'best work'. None of the three notebooks the poems were written in has survived, and it is impossible to say exactly which of them each of the poems in *Spirits in Bondage* came from. However, we know that *Spirits in Bondage* contains fourteen poems from 'The

3. ibid., p. 214.    4. ibid., pp. 220–21.    5. ibid., p. 230.

Metrical Mediations of a Cod' (of which 'Victory', 'Noon', 'Night', 'Star Bath', and 'Sonnet' are the only ones we know by name); one at least, 'Lullaby', is from the 'the reddy-brown MS book'; and the rest are from the notebook of poems written in France and the hospital. Lewis considered a number of possible pseudonyms before deciding on 'Clive Hamilton' – his own first name and his mother's family name.

The War ended on 11 November, and Lewis arrived home on 27 December 1918 to be fêted with champagne by his father and brother, Warren. He had been away since October 1917. Following a very pleasant Christmas with his family, he returned to Oxford on 13 January 1919. Some months earlier John Galsworthy had seen a typescript of the book, and during his first term back in Oxford, one of the poems, 'Death in Battle', appeared in Galsworthy's new periodical, *Reveille*, No. 3 (February 1919). For a long time now Lewis had tried to hide his atheism from his father and his brother. Neither was deceived, however, and as they waited for the book to be published they exchanged thoughts about it. Warren complained to his father in a letter of 28 January 1919 that while he knew that his brother's atheism was 'purely academic' no 'useful purpose is served by endeavouring to advertise oneself as an Atheist'.[6] Mr Lewis took a more moderate view, and writing to Warren on 9 March he said, 'He is young and he will learn in time that a man has not absolutely solved the riddle of the heavens above and the earth beneath and the waters under the earth at twenty. I am not going to slop over but I do think that if Oxford does not spoil him . . . he may write something that men would not willingly let die.'[7] *Spirits in Bondage: A Cycle of Lyrics* by 'Clive Hamilton' was published on 20 March 1919.

In 1922, while preparing for examinations in Honour Moderations, Lewis began the narrative poem, *Dymer*, on which he worked for four years. He had great hopes for *Dymer* and most of his poetic creativity went into the writing of it. It was eventually accepted by J. M. Dent and published in 1926, but Lewis did not know this when it was turned down by William Heinemann on

6. 'Lewis Papers', vol. VI, p. 84.    7. ibid., p. 98.

5 March 1926. The day after this news was received he analysed his disappointment in the pages of his diary. 'I have flattered myself', he said, 'with the idea of being among my own people when I was reading the poets and it is unpleasant to have to stand down and take my place in the crowd . . . The cure of this disease is not easy to find – except the sort of violent, surgical cure which Reality itself may be preparing for me.'[8] Reality was already dealing just as violently with Lewis's short poems. Only one of the many written during the 1920s found a publisher. Owen Barfield was assisting the Editor of the literary periodical, *The Beacon*, during the twenties, and he accepted Lewis's 'Joy' for the issue of May 1924. It is fortunate that this poem has survived because it is the author's first attempt to explain that experience of 'intense longing' which he describes in *Surprised by Joy* as the 'central' experience of his life. It is reprinted in the 'Miscellany'.

The 'central' experience reached its culmination in 1929 when Lewis was converted to Theism. It was to be another two years before he became a Christian, but the watershed for Lewis as a writer had been reached. It is tempting to say that his watershed as a poet was reached, but that would be to divide the man up, and that is certainly not what happened. The most noticeable effect of Lewis's conversion was the death of his old ambition a a poet and the emergence of a man never thereafter at a loss for the right words. Arthur Greeves had a bitter disappointment of his own in the summer of 1930 when a book he had been working on for years was turned down. Lewis wrote on 18 August to say that they were both in the same boat because God was being merciful in not allowing them a literary success later to be revealed a 'dust and ashes'. It is tempting, he said, to suppose that it would be 'ample bliss' if your book was published even if it was read only by your friends. 'This is an *absolute delusion* . . . I am *still* as disappointed an author as you. From the age of sixteen onwards I had one single ambition, from which I never wavered, in the persecution of which I spent every ounce I could, on wh. I really & deliberately staked my whole

8. *They Stand Together*, p. 383. This entry from Lewis's diary accompanies the letter to Arthur Greeves of 18 August 1930.

contentment: and I recognize myself as having unmistakably failed in it . . . Depend upon it, unless God has abandoned us, he will find means to cauterize that side somehow or other.'⁹

In his next letter, of 28 August 1930, Lewis admitted that now that he no longer regarded himself 'officially as an author' ideas had begun to 'bubble and simmer'. 'It is a very remarkable thing,' he said, 'that in the few religious lyrics which I have written during the last year, in which I had no idea of publication & at first very little idea even of showing them to friends, I have found myself impelled to take infinitely more pains, less ready to be contented with the fairly good and more determined to reach the best attainable, than ever I was in the days when I never wrote without the ardent hope of successful publication.'¹⁰

Fourteen of these religious lyrics were sent to Owen Barfield during the summer of 1930 under the general title 'Half Hours with Hamilton', and they are some of the most beautiful poems Lewis wrote. Most of these same poems were to appear a couple of years later in his semi-autobiographical *The Pilgrim's Regress* (1933). They were always Lewis's favourites of his own poems. During the early 1930s he copied, all told, thirty-eight poems into his notebook of religious lyrics. One of these thirty-eight poems, first published in *Poems*, is the one entitled 'Reason' in which he says that when imagination and reason agree in him he will be able to say 'I BELIEVE'.

In that entry of his dairy for 6 April 1926 which he sent to Arthur, Lewis said: 'I should like and like greatly to be known (and praised) by one or two friends and good judges: but I hold this as a refinement of pleasure easily foregone. If it went by another's name, so long as it was read and liked, I should be quite content.'¹¹ This really is what happened. Lewis wrote a good many poems over the next thirty years, but few of his friends would have seen them. He invariably sent a copy of his latest poem to Owen Barfield, with a note saying 'Any good?', 'Will this do?' His chief enjoyment lay in the writing of poetry. Most of Lewis's prose came from his head almost exactly as it appears on the printed page, with only an occasional

9. ibid., pp. 378–79.    10. ibid., p. 385.    11. ibid, p. 382.

word being changed. It was not like this with his poetry. They went through endless revisions, the best example of which are the religious lyrics of 1930 which he was still revising up to the time he died.

If Lewis was satisfied with a poem he would publish it. A few appeared in his own name but, from 1934 to 1957, most of his poems were published in *The Oxford Magazine* or *Punch* under the pseudonym Nat Whilk (Anglo-Saxon for 'I know not whom') or 'N.W.'. '"Poetry" with the Eliots and Audens has become such a horror,' he wrote to his brother on 20 July 1940, 'that the real thing now mainly survives in verse not intended to be fully serious – e.g. there is more real poetry in *Punch* now than in the high brow periodicals.' Then, shortly before he was made Professor of Medieval and Renaissance English at Cambridge in 1954, he began collecting his poems, published and unpublished, towards eventual publication in a volume to be called *Young King Cole, and other Pieces*. He began going through the three notebooks of poems written in the thirties, forties and fifties and revising some of them extensively.

Following his marriage to a dying woman in 1957, and during their three years together, Lewis gave up copying poems into a notebook, and he published only two. It was, however, the bittersweet years with Joy Lewis which led him to write those poignant love poems 'Joys That Sting', 'Old Poets Remembered', 'As the Ruin Falls' and 'Love's as Warm as Tears'. In 1963, three years after his wife died, Lewis returned to *Young King Cole*. He was still a long way from completing the task, but he was very eager to get on with it and he got as far as writing an 'Introductory Letter' which he planned to use as a Preface. This 'Introductory Letter', as I've called it, is in the form of a letter to the editor of a literary periodical, and it has never been published before.

The literary establishment has changed a good deal since 1963 and Lewis's 'Introductory Letter' is included in this volume, not as a challenge to contemporary readers, but because it is historically part of his literary output. I asked Mr Barfield if he would comment on it and he said:

He wrote it is the form of a letter because he wanted to give expression to the difference between his view of poetry and the prevailing contemporary one. He knew what poetry *is*. However, if you're going to published your own verse you don't really want at the same time to published your own *theory* of poetry. It's not appropriate. But you may want in the specially unfavourable atmosphere there was at the time the book was being prepared for publication to comment on that contemporary view and, to some extent, meet it. The letter is a criticism of a particular attitude that was very prevalent at the time. You had the period after the First War, the thirties, forties, fifties, when the fashionable attitude was amoral, or even anti-moral. The atmosphere was one of pointless ironical detachment. Lewis didn't want to write a manifesto, but by writing in the form of a letter he specifies that he had a particular end, a particular phenomenon, in view which will affect the reception of his poems. The *key* sentence in the whole thing is that in which he says 'The critic whose praise I covet and whose censure I fear but will never resent' is the one who exhibits 'the kind and degree of my failure or success' as a poet.

It remains to mention what is in the 'Miscellany'. There are, as mentioned earlier, the ten poems from the youthful 'Metrical Meditations of a Cod', and these have been dated. 'Joy' was published under the pseudonym 'Clive Hamilton' in *The Beacon* vol. III (May 1924). The Lewis brothers' father, Albert Lewis, died in 1929 while Warren was on duty in China. After his return to England the brothers decided to sell the family home in Belfast. As Warren prepared to make his final visit to 'Little Lea' in June 1930 Lewis composed and sent him 'Leaving For Ever the Home of One's Youth'. It was published in *Occasional Poets: An Anthology*, edited by Richard Adams (1986).

'Essence' was found in a work entitled *Fear No More: A Book of Poems for the Present Time by living English Poets* (1940) in which all the poems are anonymous. Six copies were printed with a list of the authors' names for the National Libraries, and I discovered from the copy in the Bodleian Library that Lewis is the author of this poem. Lewis's delightful nonsense poem, 'Awake, My Lute!', which was inspired by the Lord Chancellor's nightmare ('When you're lying awake with a dismal headache, and repose is taboo'd by anxiety') from *Iolanthe* – was originally published in *The Atlantic*

*Monthly*, CLXXII (November 1943). 'Consolation' has never been published before and was probably written about 1945. 'Finchley Avenue', in which Lewis seems to be remembering his childhood home, 'Little Lea', was written about 1950, and it too has been published in *Occasional Poets*.

Sometimes before his marriage Lewis wrote two versions of an 'Epitaph'. The one he planned to use in *Young King Cole* appears as Epitaph 17 at the end of *Poems*. When Joy read this poem she knew she was dying and she asked that it be used as her epitaph. In July 1963 Lewis revised the epitaph with her in mind and arranged for it be cut into marble and placed in the Oxford Crematorium. That same poem is being published for the first time in the 'Miscellany of Additional Poems'.

My sincere thanks to Owen Barfield for all the help he has given me over these last thirty years. No matter how occupied he has been with his own work he has never failed to break off when I needed his advice, or simply because I wanted to talk. 'Barfield cannot talk on any subject without illuminating it', Lewis wrote in 1962. Nothing could be more appropriate than the decision of the Estate of C. S. Lewis to dedicate the *Collected Poems* to him.

WALTER HOOPER
*Oxford*
*25 January 1994*

# INTRODUCTORY LETTER

Dear Madam (or Sir) – Spectacles made for one man will suit another only by a lucky accident; and since there was no thought of pleasing you when the pieces in this volume were written it is a hundred to one against your finding it any pleasure to read them. This letter, well-used, will enable you to write a very passable review without that laborious preliminary.

You may safely and even truly say that the author is out of touch with all the dominant trends of contemporary literature. If you don't think the word too *usé*, you can call him an escapist. From what or into what or why he is escaping, I think you had better not discuss; your readers don't expect it and that sort of thing may easily land one in difficulties.

Poetic Diction and even archaism ought certainly to be among the charges you bring. But I wouldn't line the author up with other archaists unless you have really read them. And remember that 'Wardour Street', beside being a bit stale, is an expression that has strings attached to it.

This, with a quotation or so – you can choose them blind, for I assure you there is no part of the book you will dislike much more than another – would almost do for a short notice. If, however, you are paid by the inch or your employer for any reason wants to fill up space, you could say that the author seems mainly interested in phonetic patterns: consonances, assonances, internal or inbedded rhymes, and all that. An internal rhyme is a thing like 'exCEPT at the making of Eve Adam SLEPT': an inbedded rhyme, one like 'In CRIMSon shade their LIMBS are laid'. If you are short of matter this distinction should be good for a hundred and odd words. You may trot it out as your own if you like, for I won't give you away and those who read your review will obviously not be likely to read the book. A reference to Skaldic metres might come in at this point.

There are, to be sure, people who really know about them, but they again will not be among your readers.

I wouldn't, however, go on to say anything of your own about metres. Your education has been neglected on that side and you would probably mistake for *vers libre* the pieces which are really in the strictest and most complicated metres of all. Anyway, your public has no interest in the subject.

For safety's sake don't embark on an imaginary history of how, when or why the things were written. Keep that for dead authors. When you apply it to the living there are people who know whether the results are right or wrong. I have never once known them to be right.

For the same reason I'd avoid *Quellenforschung*. It involves biographical, and indeed literary, knowledge which you don't possess. But though you should keep clear of the thing there is no reason why you shouldn't use the word. For example, it would be quite effective – on the basis of this very passage – to say, 'Lewis, for reasons not hard to conjecture, deprecates *Quellenforschung*'. This sentence, by the way, has the advantage that if there is any confusion in the printing-house (or elsewhere) between *deprecate* and *depreciate*, it won't really matter. Whichever turns up in print, you can defend it.

I mean, of course, defend it against your own kind. You needn't bother about defending it against me, for I have one great virtue as an author – I never answer criticism. Falsehoods about matter of fact (if they meet my eyes) I do; and it is only fair to your profession to say that no one whom I caught lying about me ever lied about me again. Of my dead friends you had better be more careful than of me. I have been thought to have a pretty vein in spurgalling a ghoul.

With myself, on the other hand, you can be (barring fact) pretty free. The psychological and sociological line in denigration is generally the most reliable. Why not invent a new group to which you can assign me – say, The Angry Old Men? Though I may not be so angry – not, anyway, with things in general – as the Young Men, I have perhaps a better claim to Age than some of them to Youth. But whatever line you take, have a good time, please your own fancy, and don't waste any pains trying to find out the particular types of mud you think I would most dislike. I don't belong to a press-cutting concern and consequently I see reviews of my own work only by accident. It would be a shame if any carefully concocted venom thus went to waste.

It is of course just possible that some one critic who reads this letter may be of quite a different sort from those I have been trying to help: may love and understand what I have attempted and may be concerned not at all with me as a person or a type but solely with diagnosing and exhibiting the kind and degree of my failure or success. That is the critic whose praise I covet and whose censure I fear but will never resent. There is no need to elaborate the point. We understand one another.

For the rest – for you, the far more probable critic – I have a kindlier feeling than you may suppose. Wilfred Shadbolt in the comic opera had not become an assistant tormentor because he liked assistant tormenting. You are not a reviewer for the fun of a thing, and if you rose much above the orthodox contemporary type of work in this kind you would probably lose your job. Your trade is dreadful as gathering samphire and I wish you the speedy chance of a better one with all my heart.

Yours etc.

C. S. LEWIS

1963

# POEMS

# PREFACE

C. S. Lewis published his first poem, 'Quam Bene Saturno', in tne Cherbourg School Magazine of 1913. The young classical student writes 'after Tibullus' as many others have done. He begins:

> Alas! what happy days were those
> When Saturn ruled a peaceful race ...

and ends:

> But now ... With Jove our haughty lord
> No peace we know but many a wound:
> And famine, slaughter, fire and sword
> With grim array our path surround.

He was then fourteen. He never tired of the Classical Poets; throughout his life we find him happy to use Pagan deities as spiritual symbols. Occasionally he attempts the metres of the Latin lyrics in English: Sapphics (p. 16), Asclepiads (p. 47), Alcaics (p. 55), Hendecasyllabics (p. 92), not to mention the 'Scazons' of p. 132 which are not in strict classical metre, but loosely intimate the general effect.

Lewis' ambition to become a great poet really began with the publication in 1919 (when he was twenty) of *Spirits in Bondage: A Cycle of Lyrics* under the transparent pseudonym of Clive Hamilton (his own first name and his mother's maiden name). The poems abound in what he called 'thoughtful wishing' (not wishful thinking) and his purpose is clear in the opening lyric:

> In my coracle of verses I will sing of lands unknown,
> Flying from the scarlet city where a Lord that knows no pity
> Mocks the broken people praying round his iron throne,
> – Sing about the Hidden Country fresh and full of quiet green,
> Sailing over seas uncharted to a port that none has seen.

Seven years later, as a Fellow of Magdalen College, Oxford, Clive

Hamilton published *Dymer* (1926), a long narrative poem in nine cantos of rhyme royal. In the Preface to the second edition (1950) Lewis recalls much of the psychological motivation behind *Dymer*. He was an idealist and an atheist when he wrote the poem. There were other experiments in writing long poems but none were ever published. *Till We Have Faces* was, in its infancy, a poem; it grew into a novel.

Lewis, however, continued to write short lyrics all his life. Many are included in his first prose work, *The Pilgrim's Regress* (1933). Others were published during the thirties in the *Oxford Magazine* under a new pseudonym – Nat Whilk (Anglo-Saxon for 'I know not whom'). But his voice had changed: Lewis became a Christian in 1929. And 'the new voice', says Owen Barfield, 'with its unmistakable note of magisterial humility, when it spoke in 1933 in *The Pilgrim's Regress*, was already the voice of the author of *Screwtape*, of the *Personal Heresy*, of the *Broadcast Talks*, of the Founding President of the Socratic Club'. As for his other poems, though many were published they are not easy to come by. Twenty-four appeared (between 1946 and 1954) in the pages of *Punch* over the initials 'N.W.' There were also occasional contributions to the *Spectator*, *Time and Tide* and other magazines. Their history is recorded in the appendix to this volume.

A sampling of all Lewis' works will reveal the same man in his poetry as in his clear and sparkling prose. His wonderful imagination is the guiding thread. It is continuously at work – in his first school poem, through *Screwtape*, literary criticism, planetary romances, and fairy-tales. It is basic to the man. And this is why, I think, his admirers find it so pleasant to be instructed by him in subjects they have hitherto cared so little for. Everything he touched had his kind of magic about it. His poetry, like his prose, is teeming with ideas and the good fruits of humour, wit, common sense, and scholarship.

The reader will be struck by the range of these poems: there is room for God and the Pagan deities, unicorns and space-ships. Lewis did not, of course, believe in the factual existence of Dryads (any more than Spenser or Milton); nor did he believe in their non-existence as a nihilist would. The whole rich and genial universe of mythological beings – giants, dragons, paradises, gods – were to him abbreviated symbols of qualities present in the world, or as Lewis in one place calls them, 'words of a language which speaks the else unspeakable'. When Subjectivists throw the gods out with the bath-water they empty out truths we cannot recover. 'Nature', he says, 'has that in her which compels us to invent giants: and only giants will do'. We find, as well, a defence for talking-beasts in 'Impenitence' where Lewis calls them:

> Masks for Man, cartoons, parodies by Nature
> Formed to reveal us.

Now let me say something about the compiling of this book. Lewis began collecting his poems over ten years ago for a volume to be called *Young King Cole and other Pieces*. Some poems, including two from *The Pilgrim's Regress*, had been typed; others, added later, were in his handwriting. They were in no particular order. It was not always easy to determine his final version of a poem, especially if there were slightly different versions or if the poem had already appeared in print. Nor is it clear that the selection he had made represented a considered judgement on his part; for, as I discovered in conversation with him, he simply did not know what he had written. Anyone who had lived in his house could have understood this. Although Lewis owned a huge library, he possessed few of his own works. His phenomenal memory recorded almost everything he had read *except* his own writings – an appealing fault. Often, when I quoted lines from his own poems he would ask who the author was. He was a very great scholar, but not expert in the field of C. S. Lewis.

I have, therefore, felt justified in collecting everything I could find among his literary remains and in following my judgement as to what should be printed. I found some poems scribbled on scraps of paper or in the flyleaves of books. Others came from notebooks and are at least as old as the poems in *The Pilgrim's Regress*. As most of these had never been given titles, I usually drew titles from among the lines. Even the headings for the five Parts are taken from Lewis' own works. The present collection excludes, however, his own youthful publications of poetry *Spirits in Bondage* and *Dymer*, but includes the poems scattered through his first prose work, *The Pilgrim's Regress*, as well as subsequent pieces published in periodicals. I have chosen to arrange the poems more or less topically rather than attempt a chronological ordering. This is because I often had little else to go by except Lewis' handwriting and, too, I know from experience that he was continually revising them.

While I was his secretary he sometimes used to dictate poems. Even after he thought one was completed he might suggest a change here. Then a change there. Because of this, I warn readers from attempting to date his poems on internal evidence. For instance, the poem which in this volume is entitled 'To A Friend' was originally written 'To C.W.' and later published (1942) as 'To G.M.' It is best to fight shy of what Lewis himself called the Personal Heresy': reading a man's works as autobiography.

The fact that he did not published these poems during his lifetime suggests that Lewis was hesitant about their publication. He knew his poems were very unlike most contemporary verse. Because of this, he could not be certain of the reaction of his readers. The answer is not far to seek. In the poem, 'A Confession', Lewis says with ironical disappointment:

> I am so coarse, the things the poets see
> Are obstinately invisible to me.
> For twenty years I've stared my level best
> To see if evening – any evening – would suggest
> A patient etherized upon a table;
> In vain. I simply wasn't able.

Lewis found Mr Eliot's comparison of an evening to a patient on an operating table unpleasant, one example of the decay of proper feelings. He mistrusted, in fact, the free play of mere immediate experience. He believed, rather, that man's attitudes and actions should be governed by, what he calls in the same poem, Stock Responses (e.g. love is sweet, death bitter, and virtue lovely). Man must, for his own safety and pleasure, be taught to copy the Stock Responses in hopes that he may, by willed imitation, make the proper responses. He found this perfectly summed up in Aristotle's 'We learn how to do things by doing the things we are learning to do.' The concern is expressed, directly or indirectly, in almost all of Lewis' books, but most clearly in his defence of Milton's style (*A Preface to 'Paradise Lost'*, Ch. VIII). His belief that poetry did not need to be eccentric to enrich a response and of 'being normal without being vulgar', one of the characteristics which distinguish him from many contemporary poets, made him think he might be classed as an Angry Old Man. If so, he conceded that he was much less angry with things in general than are the Young Men, and having perhaps the better claim to Age than some do to Youth.

It is possible that some who have read those poems which have appeared in periodicals will be confused by his revisions and new titles. Because of this, I have appended to this volume a list of the published poems, indicating (1) whether they have been revised; (2) their original titles, if different; and (3) their original sources. This apparatus is not meant to suggest that Lewis had high pretensions about his poetry. It most certainly means, on the other hand, that for me this has been one of those rare jobs in which labour is more pleasure than anything else.

I want to thank the editors of *The Cambridge Review*, *The Cherwell*, *The Magazine of Fantasy and Science Fiction*, *The Month*, *The Oxford Magazine*, *Punch*, *The Spectator*, *Time and Tide* and *The Times Literary Supplement* for permission to reprint some of the poems in this book; they are acknowledged individually in the appendix. I am indebted to Mr Charles Böhmer whose initiative and generosity made this venture possible, to Mr George Sayer for lending me poems given him by Lewis, to Mr Owen Barfield for his useful criticism, and to Dr and Mrs Austin Farrer for their encouragement and wise counsel. Finally, I am deeply grateful to Major W. H. Lewis for allowing me the honour of editing his brother's poems.

WALTER HOOPER
*Oxford*
*1964*

# CONTENTS

## PART III: A LARGER WORLD

## PART IV: NOON'S INTENSITY

# Part 1

# THE HIDDEN COUNTRY

# A CONFESSION

I am so coarse, the things the poets see
Are obstinately invisible to me.
For twenty years I've stared my level best
To see if evening – any evening – would suggest
A patient etherized upon a table;
In vain. I simply wasn't able.
To me each evening looked far more
Like the departure from a silent, yet a crowded, shore
Of a ship whose freight was everything, leaving behind
Gracefully, finally, without farewells, marooned mankind.

Red dawn behind a hedgerow in the east
Never, for me, resembled in the least
A chilblain on a cocktail-shaker's nose;
Waterfalls don't remind me of torn underclothes,
Nor glaciers of tin-cans. I've never known
The moon look like a hump-backed crone –
Rather, a prodigy  even now
Nor naturalized, a riddle glaring from the Cyclops' brow
Of the cold world, reminding me on what a place
I crawl and cling, a planet with no bulwarks, out in space.

Never the white sun of the wintriest day
Struck me as *un crachat d'estaminet.*
I'm like that odd man Wordsworth knew, to whom
A primrose was a yellow primrose, one whose doom
Keeps him forever in the list of dunces,
Compelled to live on stock responses,
Making the poor best that I can
Of dull things . . . peacocks, honey, the Great Wall, Aldebaran,
Silver weirs, new-cut grass, wave on the beach, hard gem,
The shapes of horse and woman, Athens, Troy, Jerusalem.

# IMPENITENCE

All the world's wiseacres in arms against them
Shan't detach my heart for a single moment
From the man-like beasts of the earthy stories –
    Badger or Moly.


Rat the oarsman, neat Mrs Tiggy Winkle,
Benjamin, pert Nutkin, or (ages older)
Henryson's shrill Mouse, or the Mice the Frogs once
    Fought with in Homer.


Not that I'm so craz'd as to think the creatures
Do behave that way, nor at all deluded
By some half-false sweetness of early childhood
    Sharply remembered.


Look again. Look well at the beasts, the true ones.
Can't you see? . . . cool primness of cats, or coney's
Half indignant stare of amazement, mouse's
    Twinkling adroitness.


Tipsy bear's rotundity, toad's complacence . . .
Why! they all cry out to be used as symbols,
Masks for Man, cartoons, parodies by Nature
    Formed to reveal us

Each in each, not fiercely but in her gentlest
Vein of household laughter. And if the love so
Raised – it will, no doubt – splashes over on the
    Actual archtypes,

Who's the worse for that? Marry, gup! Begone, you
Fusty kill-joys, new Manichaens! Here's a
Health to Toad Hall, here's to the Beaver doing
Sums with the Butcher!


# A CLICHÉ CAME OUT OF ITS CAGE

## 1

You said 'The world is going back to Paganism'. Oh bright
Vision! I saw our dynasty in the bar of the House
Spill from their tumblers a libation to the Erinyes,
And Leavis with Lord Russell wreathed in flowers, heralded with
    flutes,
Leading white bulls to the cathedral of the solemn Muses
To pay where due the glory of their latest theorem.
Hestia's fire in every flat, rekindled, burned before
The Lardergods. Unmarried daughters with obedient hands
Tended it. By the hearth the white-arm'd venerable mother
*Domum servabat, lanam faciebat.* Duly at the hour
Of sacrifice their brothers came, silent, corrected, grave
Before their elders; on their downy cheeks easily the blush
Arose (it is the mark of freemen's children) as they trooped,
Gleaming with oil, demurely home from the palaestra or the dance.
Walk carefully, do not wake the envy of the happy gods,
Shun Hubris. The middle of the road, the middle sort of men,
Are best. Aidos surpasses gold. Reverence for the aged
Is wholesome as seasonable rain, and for a man to die
Defending the city in battle is a harmonious thing.
Thus with magistral hand the Puritan Sophrosune
Cooled and schooled and tempered our uneasy motions;
Heathendom came again, the circumspection and the holy fears . . .
You said it. Did you mean it? Oh inordinate liar, stop.

[17]

Or did you mean another kind of heathenry?
Think, then, that under heaven-roof the little disc of the earth,
Fortified Midgard, lie encircled by the ravening Worm.
Over its icy bastions of giant and troll
Look in, ready to invade it. The Wolf, admittedly, is bound;
But the bond will break, the Beast run free. The weary gods,
Scarred with old wounds, the one-eyed Odin, Tyr who has lost a
    hand,
Will limp to their stations for the last defence. Make it your hope
To be counted worthy on that day to stand beside them;
For the end of man is to partake of their defeat and die
His second, final death in good company. The stupid, strong
Unteachable monsters are certain to be victorious at last,
And every man of decent blood is on the losing side.
Take as your model the tall women with yellow hair in plaits
Who walked back into burning houses to die with men,
Or him who as the death spear entered into his vitals
Made critical comments on its workmanship and aim.
Are these the Pagans you spoke of? Know your betters and crouch,
    dogs;
You that have Vichy-water in your veins and worship the event,
Your goddess History (whom your fathers called the strumpet
    Fortune).

# PAN'S PURGE

I dreamt that all the planning of peremptory humanity
   Had crushed Nature finally beneath the foot of Man;
Birth-control and merriment, Earth completely sterilized,
   Bungalow and fun-fair, had fulfilled our Plan;
But the lion and the unicorn were sighing at the funeral,
    Crying at the funeral,
   Sobbing at the funeral of the god Pan.


And the elephant was crying. The pelican in his piety
   Struck his feathered bosom till he blood ran,
And howling at humanity the owl and iguanodon,
   The bittern and the buffalo, their dirge began,
But dangerously, suddenly, a strange ecstatic shuddering,
    A change that set me shuddering
   Through all the wailful noises of the beasts ran.


No longer were they sorrowful, but stronger and more horrible,
   It had only been a rumour of the death of Pan.
The scorpions and the mantichores and corpulent tarantulas
   Were closing in around me, hissing *Long live Pan!*
And forth with rage unlimited the Northwind drew his scimitar,
    In wrath with ringing scimitar
   He came, with sleet and shipwreck, for the doom of Man.


And now, descending, ravening, loud and large, the avalanche,
   And after it the earthquake, was loosed upon Man.
Towering and cloven-hoofed, the power of Pan came over us,
   Stamped, bit, tore, broke. It was the end of Man;
Except where saints and savages were kept from his ravaging,
    And crept out when the ravaging
   Was ended, on an empty earth. The new world began.

A small race – a smiling heaven – all round the silences
   Returned; there was comfort for corrected Man.
Flowered turf had swallowed up the towered cities; following
   His flocks and herds where nameless, untainted rivers ran,
Leisurely he pondered, at his pleasure wandering,
    Measurelessly wandering . . .
   Clear, on the huge pastures, the young voice of Man.

## NARNIAN SUITE

### 1

*March for Strings, Kettledrums, and Sixty-three Dwarfs*

With plucking pizzicato and the prattle of the kettledrum
We're trotting into battle mind a clatter of accoutrement;
Our beards are big as periwigs and trickle with opopanax,
And trinketry and treasure twinkle out on every part of us –
    (Scrape! Tap! The fiddle and the kettledrum).

The chuckle-headed humans think we're only petty poppetry
And all our battle-tackle nothing more than pretty bric-a-brac;
But a little shrub has prickles, and they'll soon be in a pickle if
A scud of dwarfish archery has crippled all their cavalry –
    (Whizz! Twang! The quarrel and the javelin).

And when the tussle thickens we can writhe and wriggle under it;
The dagger-point'll tickle 'em, and grab and grip'll grapple 'em,
And trap and trick'll trouble 'em and tackle 'em and topple 'em
Till they're huddled, all be-diddled, in the middle of our caperings –
    (Dodge! Jump! The wriggle and the summersault).

When we've scattered 'em and peppered 'em with pebbles from our
                                    catapults
We'll turn again in triumph and by crannies and by crevices
Go back to where the capitol and cradle of our people is,
Our forges and our furnaces, the caverns of the earth –
      (Gold! Fire! The anvil and the smithying).

## 2

*March for Drum, Trumpet, and Twenty-one Giants*

            With stumping stride in pomp and pride
            We come to thump and floor ye;
            We'll bump your lumpish heads today
            And tramp your ramparts into clay,
            And as we stamp and romp and play
            Our trump'll below before us –
*(crescendo)*      Oh tramp it, tramp it, tramp it, trumpet, trumpet
                                  blow before us!

            We'll grind and break and bind and take
            And plunder ye and pound ye!
            With trundled rocks and bludgeon blow,
            You dunderheads, we'll dint ye so
            You'll blunder and run blind, as though
            By thunder stunned, around us –
By thunder, thunder, thunder, thunder stunned around us!

            Ho! tremble town and tumble down
            And crumble shield and sabre!
            Your kings will mumble and look pale,
            Your horses stumble or turn tail,
            Your skimble-scamble counsels fail,
            So rumble drum belaboured –
*(Diminuendo)* Oh rumble, rumble, rumble, rumble, rumble drum
                                 belaboured!

# THE MAGICIAN AND THE DRYAD

MAGICIAN

Out of your dim felicity of leaves, oh Nymph appear,
Answer me in soft-showery voice, attempt the unrooted dance
– My art shall sponsor the enormity. Now concentrate,
Arouse, where in your vegetative heart it drowses deep
In seminal sleep, your feminine response. *Conjuro te*
*Per Hecates essentiam et noctis silentia,*
Breaking by Trivia's name your prison of bark. Beautiful, awake.

DRYAD

Risen from the deep lake of my liberty, into your prison
She has come, cruel commander.

MAGICIAN

               I have given speech to the dumb.
Will you not thank me, silver lady?

DRYAD

             Oh till now she drank
With thirst of myriad mouths the bursting cataracts of the sun,
The drizzle of gentler stars, an indivisible small rain.
Wading the dark earth, made of earth and light, cradled in air,
All that she was, she was all over. Now the mask you call
A Face has blotted out the ambient hemisphere's embrace;
Her light is screwed into twin nodules of tormenting sight
Searing divisions tear her into five. She cannot hear
But only see, the moon; the earth has no taste; she cannot breathe
At every branch vibrations of the sky. For a dome of severance,
A helmet, a dark, rigid box of bone, has overwhelmed
Her hair . . . that was her lungs . . . that was her nerves . . . that
    kissed the air.
Crushed in a brain, her thought that circled coolly in every vein

Turns into poison, thickens like a man's ferments and burns.
She was at peace when she was in her unity. Oh now release
And let her out into the seamless world, make her forget.

MAGICIAN
Be free. Relapse. And so she vanishes. And now the tree
Grows barer every moment. The leaves fall. A killing air,
Sighing from the country of Man, has withered it. The tree will die.


## THE TRUE NATURE OF GNOMES

Paracelsus somewhere in his writings tell us
   A gnome moves through earth like an arrow in the air,
At home like a fish within the seamless, foamless
   Liberty of the water that yields to it everywhere.

Beguiled with pictures, I fancied in my childhood
   Subterranean rivers beside glimmering wharfs,
Hammers upon anvils, pattering and yammering,
   Torches and tunnels, the cities of the dwarfs;

But in perfect blackness underneath the surface,
   In a silence unbroken till the planet cracks,
Their sinewy bodies through the dense continuum
   Move without resistance and leave no tracks.

Gravel, marl, blue clay – all's one to travel in;
   Only one obstacle can impede a gnome –
A cave or a mine-shaft. Not their very bravest
   Would venture across it for a short cut home.

There is the unbridgeable. To a gnome the air is
   Utter vacuity. If he thrust out his face
Into a cavern, his face would break in splinters,
   Bursting as a man would burst in interstellar space.

With toiling lungs a gnome can breathe the soil in,
  Rocks are like a headwind, stiff against his chest,
Chief 'midst his pleasures is the quiet leaf mould,
  Like air in meadowy valleys when the wind's at rest.

Like silvan freshness are the lodes of silver,
  Cold, clammy, fog-like, are the leaden veins
Those of gold are prodigally sweet like roses,
  Gems stab coolly like the small spring rains.


## THE BIRTH OF LANGUAGE

How near his sire's careering fires
Must Mercury the planet run;
What wave of heat must lave and beat
That shining suburb of the Sun

Whose burning flings supernal things
Like spindrift from his stormy crown;
He throws and shakes in rosy flakes
Intelligible virtues down,

And landing there, the candent air
A transformation on them brings,
Makes each a god of speech with rod
Enwreathed and sandals fledged with wings.

Due west (the Sun's behest so runs)
They seek the wood where flames are trees;
In crimson shade their limbs are laid
Besides the pure quicksilver seas,

Where thick with notes of liquid throats
The forest melody leaps and runs

Till night lets robe the lightless globe
With darkness and with distant suns.

Awake they spring and shake the wing;
And on the trees whose trunks are flames
They find like fruit (with rind and root
And fronds of fire) their proper names.

They taste. They burn with haste. They churn.
With upright plumes the sky's abyss;
Far, far below, the arbours glow
Where once they felt Mercurial bliss.

They ache and freeze through vacant seas
Of night. Their nimbleness and youth
Turns lean and frore; their meaning more,
Their being less. Fact shrinks to truth.

They reach this Earth. There each has birth
Miraculous, a word made breath,
Lucid and small for use in all
Man's daily needs; but dry like death.

So dim below these symbols show,
Bony and abstract every one.
Yet if true verse but left the curse,
They feel in dreams their native Sun.

# THE PLANETS

Lady LUNA, in light canoe,
By friths and shallows of fretted cloudland
Cruises monthly; with chrism of dews
And drench of dream, a drizzling glamour,
Enchants us – the cheat! changing sometime
A mind to madness, melancholy pale,
Bleached with gazing on her blank count'nance
Orb'd and ageless. In earth's bosom
The shower of her rays, sharp-feathered light
Reaching downward, ripens silver,
Forming and fashioning female brightness,
– Metal maidenlike. Her moist circle
Is nearest earth. Next beyond her
MERCURY marches; – madcap rover,
Patron of pilf'rers. Pert quicksilver
His gaze begets, goblin mineral,
Merry multitude of meeting selves,
Same but sundered. From the soul's darkness,
With wreathèd wand, words he marshals,
Guides and gathers them – gay bellwether
Of flocking fancies. His flint has struck
The spark of speech from spirit's tinder,
Lord of language! He leads forever
The spangle and splendour, sport that mingles
Sound with senses, in subtle pattern,
Words in wedlock, and wedding also
Of thing with thought. In the third region
VENUS voyages . . . but my voice falters;
Rude rime-making wrongs her beauty,
Whose breasts and brow, and her breath's sweetness
Bewitch the worlds. Wide-spread the reign
Of her secret sceptre, in the sea's caverns,

In grass growing, and grain bursting,
Flower unfolding, and flesh longing,
And shower falling sharp in April.
The metal copper in the mine reddens
With muffled brightness, like muted gold,
By her fingers form'd. Far beyond her
The heaven's highway hums and trembles,
Drums and dindles, to the driv'n thunder
Of SOL's chariot, whose sword of light
Hurts and humbles; beheld only
Of eagle's eye. When his arrow glances
Through mortal mind, mists are parted
And mild as morning the mellow wisdom
Breathes o'er the breast, broadening eastward
Clear and cloudless. In a clos'd garden
(Unbound her burden) his beams foster
Soul in secret, where the spoil puts forth
Paradisal palm, and pure fountains
Turn and re-temper, touching coolly
The uncomely common to cordial gold;
Whose ore also, in earth's matrix,
Is print and pressure of his proud signet
On the wax of the world. He is the worshipp'd male,
The earth's husband, all-beholding,
Arch-chemic eye. But other country
Dark with discord dins beyond him,
With noise of nakers, neighing of horses,
Hammering of harness. A haughty god
MARS mercenary, makes there his camp
And flies his flag; flaunts laughingly
The graceless beauty; grey-eyed and keen,
– Blond insolence – of his blithe visage
Which is hard and happy. He hews the act,
The indifferent deed with dint of his mallet
And his chisel of choice; achievement comes not
Unhelped by him; – hired gladiator

Of evil and good. All's one to Mars,
The wrong righted, rescued meekness,
Or trouble in trenches, with trees splintered
And birds banished, banks fill'd with gold
And the liar made lord. Like handiwork
He offers to all – earns his wages
And whistles the while. White-feathered dread
Mars has mastered. His metal's iron
That was hammered through hands into holy cross,
Cruel carpentry. He is cold and strong,
Necessity's son. Soft breathes the air
Mild, and meadowy, as we mount further
Where rippled radiance rolls about us
Moved with music – measureless the waves'
Joy and jubilee. It is JOVE'S orbit,
Filled and festal, faster turning
With arc ampler. From the Isles of Tin
Tyrian traders, in trouble steering
Came with his cargoes; the Cornish treasure
That his ray ripens. Of wrath ended
And woes mended, of winter passed
And guilt forgiven, and good fortune
Jove is master; and of jocund revel,
Laughter of ladies. The lion-hearted,
The myriad-minded, men like the gods,
Helps and heroes, helms of nations
Just and gentle, are Jove's children,
Work his wonders. On his wide forehead
Calm and kingly, no care darkens
Nor wrath wrinkles: but righteous power
And leisure and largess their loose splendours
Have wrapped around him – a rich mantle
Of ease and empire. Up far beyond
Goes SATURN silent in the seventh region,
The skirts of the sky. Scant grows the light,
Sickly, uncertain (the Sun's finger

Daunted with darkness). Distance hurts us,
And the vault severe of vast silence;
Where fancy fails us, and fair language,
And love leaves us, and light fails us
And Mars fails us, and the mirth of Jove
Is as tin tinkling. In tattered garment,
Weak with winters, he walks forever
A weary way, wide round the heaven,
Stoop'd and stumbling, with staff groping,
The lord of lead. He is the last planet
Old and ugly. His eye fathers
Pale pestilence, pain of envy,
Remorse and murder. Melancholy drink
(For bane or blessing) of bitter wisdom
He pours for his people, a perilous draught
That the lip loves not. We leave all things
To reach the rim of the round welkin,
Heaven's hermitage, high and lonely.


## PINDAR SANG

Pindar stood with his chorus on the dancing floor. The stern poet
Uttered his dark glory. Light as a flight of tumbling birds
Was the dipping and soaring of his syllables and the wheeling maze.
Demure as virgins, young men of noble houses, trained and severe,
Strongly as if it were a battle and resolutely danced his ode;
Their faces rigid, but their limbs and garments flowed like water.

'Unless a god in secret helps the work, trouble and skill
Are unavailing; the laborious plodder's wages are oblivion,
For a soul's weight is born with her. My wisdom is the birth of
    heaven;
In heaven itself the everlasting gods dare not begin
A feast or dance without the favour and assent of the grave Charites.

'For gods and men are of one stock and came of the same womb
Though an utter separation is between them, and we are nothing
While their unshakable, eternal floor is the firmament of bronze.
They look down; they behold the isle of Delos far below,
Set like a star amid the deep-blue world's level expanse.

'But we are tethered to Hope that will promise anything without
    blushing,
And the flowing water of foreknowledge is far away beyond our
    reach.
Therefore neither ashore nor in the hollow ships will any praise
Be given to an act on which the doer does not stake his life.
(At Pindus the glory of the Dorian spear burst into flower.)
And we live for a day. What are we? What are we not? A man
Is a dream about a shadow. Only when a brightness falls from
    heaven
Can human splendour expand and glow and mortal days grow soft.
'Not even to Kadmos though a peer for Gods, not to the Aiakid
Peleus, was there allowed a perfect, whole, unslippery life;
Though these were fortunate, men say, beyond all human bounds
And heard the gold-drown'd Moses singing on their marriage day.
Over the mountain and to seven-gated Thebes the song
Drew near when deep-dark-eyed Harmonia became Kadmos' bride,
And Peleus took the Nereid Thetis, and had gods for guests.
He also had sorrow afterwards for Achilles' sake, his son,
And Kadmos, weeping for his daughter; even though the Father of
    the skies
Had lain in Semele's desired bed and white embrace.

'Take the god's favour when it comes. Now from one quarter, now
From another, the wing'd weathers ride above us. Not for long,
If it grows heavy with goodness, will fortune remain good.

'Once over Lerna a shower of snow turned into flakes of gold;
Once, following the doe of the Pleiades whose horns were
    charactered with gold,

Herakles hunted far beyond the Ister till he found
A land that lies at the other side of the North Wind. And he stood
Gazing upon the trees of that country; he was struck with sweet
    desire.
But do not therefore imagine that ever you, by land or sea,
Will find the miraculous road into the Hyperborean place.
Of unattainable longings sour is the fruit; griding madness.

'Bless'd is the man who does not enter into the grave, the hollow
    earth,
Before he has seen at Eleusis the acts unspeakable which show
The end and new beginning of our life, the divine gift.
Some find the road that leads beyond the tower of Kronos, and the
    isles
Where no one labours, no one bruises the flower of his white hand
Wounding with spade or oar the parsimonious earth or bitter sea.
Golden are the flowers they pick for garlands in the righteous wood.
'But the voice of the Pierides is hateful to all the enemies of Zeus,
And the melody that makes drowsy with delight the eagle on his
    sceptre
Is torture to those who lie in Tartaros. Hundred-headed Typhon
Struggles in anguish as he hears it, vomiting lava and smoke.'

The heaven-descended nobles of the pure Dorian blood,
Not thinking they understood him, but silent in reverence for the
    god
And for the stern poet, heard him and understood it all.
Tears stood in their eyes because of the beauty of the young men
who danced.

# HERMIONE IN
## THE HOUSE OF PAULINA

How soft it rains, how nourishingly soft and green
Has grown the dark humility of this low house
Where sunrise never enters, where I have not seen
The moon by night nor heard the footfall of a mouse,
Nor looked on any face but yours
Nor changed my posture in my place of rest
For fifteen years – oh how this quiet cures
My pain and sucks the burning from my breast.

It sucked out all the poison of my will and drew
All hot rebellion from me, all desire to break
The silence you commanded me . . . Nothing to do,
Nothing to fear or wish for, not a choice to make,
Only to be; to hear no more
Cock-crowing duty calling me to rise,
But slowly thus to ripen laid in store
In this dim nursery near your watching eyes.

Pardon, great spirit, whose tall shape like a golden tower
Stands over me or seems upon slow wings to move,
Colouring with life my paleness, with returning power,
By sober ministrations of severest love;
Pardon, that when you brought me here,
Still drowned in bitter passion, drugged with life,
I did not know . . . pardon, I though you were
Paulina, old Antigonus' young wife.

# YOUNG KING COLE

By enemies surrounded,
All venomously minded
Against him, to hound him
  To death, there lived a king
Who was great and merry-hearted,
He ate and drank and sported,
When his wounds smarted
  He would dance and sing.

With gossiping and stories,
With possets of Canary,
With goliards and glory,
  He made the time pass;
His merriment heightened
As his territory straitened,
And his grip tightened
  On the stem of his glass

When his foes assaulted
He rose and exulted
Like a lover as he vaulted
  On his gaunt horse,
Sublime and elated,
But each time he was defeated,
For the lower gods hated him
  Without remorse.

So his realm diminished;
Overwhelmed, it varnished,
He held at the finish
  But a small river-isle;
With his queen, amid the saplings

And the green rippling,
With his Fool and his Chaplain,
  Held it for a while;

Till, breathing anger,
The heathen in their hunger
Came with clangour
  To the river banks
With their commissars and harlots,
With their bombers and their hurlers
Of flame, with their snarling
  And the rattle of their tanks.

Fast came their orders
For the last king's murder;
From the reedy borders
  The grey batteries spoke.
The long endeavour
Of those strong four lovers
Relaxed forever
  Amid stench and smoke.

From their fresh, unpolluted
Flesh there sprouted
A tree fair-fruited,
  And its smell and taste
Were big with Eden;
Every twig was laden
With gold unheeded
  In the flowery waste.

Past the gossamer and midges
Past the blossomy region
Of the bees, past the pigeons'
  Green world, towards the blue,
Past the eagles' landings

Many a league ascending,
Above Alps and Andes
    Infallibly it grew;

And it cast warm joys on
The vast horizons,
But its shadow was poison
    To the evil-eyed.
Yes: they ought to have felled it.
They were caught unshielded.
Paralysed, they beheld it;
    They despaired and died.


## THE PRODIGALITY OF FIRDAUSI

Firdausi the strong Lion among poets, lean of purse
And lean with age, had finished his august mountain of verse,
The great *Shah Nameh* gleaming-glaciered with demon wars,
Bastioned with Rustem's bitter labours and Isfendiyar's,
Shadowed with Jamshid's grief and glory as with eagles' wings,
Its foot-hills dewy-forested with the amours of kings,
Clashing with rhymes that rush like snow-fed cataracts blue
                                                    and cold;
And the king commanded to be given him an elephant's burden of
                                                    gold.

Firdausi the carved Pillar among poets was not dear
To government. They smiled at the king's word. The Grand
                                                    Vizier
Twisted his pale face, making parsimonious mouths, and said
'Send the old rhymer thirty thousand silver pounds instead –
The price of ten good vineyards and a fine Circassian girl.'
This pleased them and they called a secretarial shape, a churl,
A pick-thank without understanding and of base descent,
And bade it deliver their bounty, and with mincing paces it went.

It found the Cedar among poets in the baths that day,
At ease, discoursing with his friends. Exalted men were they,
Taking their wine and sugared roseleaves in an airy hall,
Poets or theologians or saints or warriors all
Or lovers or astronomers. Like honey-drops the speech
Distilled in apophthegms or verse from the lips of each,
On rose and predestination and heroic wars
And rhetoric, and the brevity of the life of man, and the stars.

With courtesy the Lily among poets asked it will.
The bearers laid the silver at his feet. The hall was still,
The churl grew pale. Firdausi beckoned to the Nubian slave
Who had dried their feet; to him the first ten thousand coins
                                         he gave.
Ten thousand more immediately he gave the fair-haired boy
Who waved the fan, saying 'My son, may Allah send you joy;
And in your grandson's house in unbelieving Frangistan
Make it your boast that once you spoke with the splendour of
                                         Iran.'
Lastly the Heaven of poets to the churl himself returned
The remnant. 'You look pale, my friend,' he said. 'Well have
                                         you earned
This trifle for your courtesy and for the heat of the day.'
Clutching his silver, silently, the creature slunk away,
And dogs growled as he passed and beggars spat. Laughter and
                                         shame
Wait upon all his progeny; on him, Gehenna's flame.
Immediately the discourse in the baths once more began
On the beauty of women and horses and the brevity of the life of man.

## LE ROI S'AMUSE

Jove gazed
On woven mazes
Of patterned movement as the atoms whirled.
His glance turned
Into dancing, burning
Colour-gods who rushed upon that sullen world,
Waking, re-making, exalting it anew –
Silver and purple, shrill-voiced yellow, turgid crimson, and virgin
blue.

Jove stared
On overbearing
And arching splendour of the naked rocks.
Where his gaze smote,
Hazily floated
To mount like thistledown in countless flocks,
Fruit-loving, root-loving gods, cool and green
Of feathery grasses, heather and orchard, pollen'd lily, the olive and
the bean.

Jove laughed.
Like cloven-shafted
Lightning, his laughter into brightness broke.
From every dint
Where the severed splinters
Had scattered a Sylvan or a Satyr woke;
Ounces came pouncing, dragon-people flew,
There was spirited stallion, squirrel unrespectful, clanging raven and
kangaroo.

Jove sighed.
The hoving tide of
Ocean trembled at the motion of his breath.

The sigh turned
Into white, eternal,
Radiant Aphrodite unafraid of death;
A fragrance, a vagrant unrest on earth she flung,
There was favouring and fondling and bravery and building and
                    chuckling music and suckling of the young.


Jove thought.
He strove and wrought at
A thousand clarities; from his brows sprang
With earnest mien
Stern Athene;
The cold armour on her shoulders rang.
Our sires at the fires of her lucid eyes began
To speak in symbols, to seek out causes, to name the creatures; they
                    became Man.


World and Man
Unfurled their banner –
It was gay Behemoth on a sable field.
Fresh-robed
In flesh, the ennobled
Spirits carousing in their myriads reeled;
There was frolic and holiday. Jove laughed to see
The abyss empeopled, his bliss imparted, the throng that was his and
                    no longer he.

## VITREA CIRCE

The name of Circe
Is wrongly branded
(Though Homer's verses
    Portrayed her right)
By heavy-handed
And moral persons
Misunderstanding
    Her danger bright.

She used not beauty
For man's beguiling,
She craved no suitor;
    Sea-chances brought
To her forest-silent
And crimson-fruited
And snake-green island
    Her guests unsought.

She watched those drunken
And tarry sailors
Eat nectar-junket
    And Phoenix-nests;
Each moment paler
With pride, she shrunk at
Their leering, railing,
    Salt-water jests.

They thought to pluck there
Her rosial splendour?
They thought their luck there
    Was near divine?
When the meal ended

She rose and struck them
With wand extended
   And made them swine.

With smiles and kisses
No man she tempted;
She scorned love's blisses
   And toils, until
There came, undream't of,
The tough Ulysses,
From fate exempted
   By Pallas' will.

Then flashed above her
(Poor kneeling Circe,
Her snares discovered)
   The hero's blade.
She lay at mercy,
His slave, his lover,
Forgot her curses,
   Blushed like a maid.

She'd none to warn her.
He hacked and twisted
Her hedge so thorny;
   It let him pass.
Her awful distance,
Her vestal scornings,
Were bright as crystals,
   They broke like glass.

# THE LANDING

The ship's stride faltered with her change of course, awaking us.
Suddenly I saw the land. Astern, the east was red;
Budding like a flower from the pale and rippled vacancy,
      The island rose ahead.

All, then, was true; such lands, in solid verity,
Dapple the last sea that laps against the sky;
Apple-gold, the headlands of the singing Hesperides
      On glass-clear water lie.

Once before I'd seen it, but that was from Helicon,
Clear and distinct in the circle of a lens,
Peering on tip-toes, one-eyed, through a telescope
      – Goddesses' country, never men's.

Now we were landing. Bright beasts and manifold
Came like old familiars, nosing at our knees;
Nameless their kinds – Adam's naming of the animals
      Reached not those outer seas.

Up from the shore then, benumbed with hope, we went upon
Danceable lawns and under gum-sweet wood,
Glancing ever up to where a green hill at the centre of
      The hush'd island stood.

We climbed to the top and looked over upon limitless
Waters, untravelled, further west. But the three
Daughters of Hesperus were only painted images
      Hand-fast around a tree,

And instead of the Dragon we found a brazen telescope
That burned our eyes there, flashing in the sun.

It was turned to the west. As once before on Helicon,
          We looked through it, one by one.

There, once again, I beheld it, small and perilous,
Distant beyond measure, in the circle of the lens
– But this time, surely, the true one, the Hesperides'
          Country which is not men's.

Hope died – rose again – quivered, and increased in us
The strenuous longing. We re-embarked to find
That genuine and utter West. Far astern and east of us
          The first hope sank behind.


## THE DAY WITH A WHITE MARK

All day I have been tossed and whirled in a preposterous happiness:
Was it an elf in the blood? or a bird in the brain? or even part
Of the cloudily crested, fifty-league-long, loud uplifted wave
Of a journeying angel's transit roaring over and through my heart?

My garden's spoiled, my holidays are cancelled, the omens harden;
The plann'd and unplann'd miseries deepen; the knots draw tight.
Reason kept telling me all day my mood was out of season.
It was, too. In the dark ahead the breakers only are white.

Yet I – I could have kissed the very scullery taps. The colour of
My day was like a peacock's chest. In at each sense there stole
Ripplings and dewy sprinkles of delight that with them drew
Fine threads of memory through the vibrant thickness of the soul.

As though there were transparent earths and luminous trees should
          grow there,
And shining roots worked visibly far down below one's feet,

So everything, the tick of the lock, the cock crowing in the yard
Probing my soul, woke diverse buried hearts of mine to beat,

Recalling either adolescent heights and the inaccessible
Longings and ice-sharp joys that shook my body and turned me pale,
Or humbler pleasures, chuckling as it were in the ear, mumbling
Of glee, as kindly animals talk in a children's tale.

Who knows if ever it will come again, now the day closes?
No one can give me, or take away, that key. All depends
On the elf, the bird, or the angel. I doubt if the angel himself
Is free to choose when sudden heaven in man begins or ends.


## DONKEYS' DELIGHT

Ten mortal months I courted
    A girl with bright hair,
Unswerving in my service
    As the old lovers were.
Almost she had learned to call me
    Her dear love. But then,
One moment changed the omens,
    She was cold again.
For carelessly, unfairly,
    With one glance of his eyes,
A gay, light-hearted sailor
    Bore away the prize,
Unbought, which I had sought with
    Many gifts and sighs.

In stern disdain I turned to
    The Muses' service then,
To seek how the unspeakable

[43]

Could be fixed by a pen,
Not to flinch though the ink that
    I must use, they said,
Was my dearest blood, nearest
    My heart, the richest red.
I obeyed them, I made them
    Many a costly lay,
Till carelessly, unfairly,
    A boy passed that way
Who set ringing with his singing
    All the fields and lanes;
They gave him their favour,
    Lost were all my pains.


Then I passed to a Master
    Who is higher in repute,
Trusting to find justice
    At the world's root.
With rigid fast and vigil,
    Silence, and shirt of hair,
The narrow way to Paradise
    I walked with care.
But carelessly, unfairly,
    At the eleventh hour there came,
Reckless and feckless,
    Without a single claim,
A dare-devil, a ne'er-do-well
    Who smelled of shag and gin;
Before me (and far warmer
    Was his welcome) he went in.


I stood still in the chill
    Of the Great Morning,
Aghast. Then at last
    – Oh, I was late learning –

I repented, I entered
   Into the excellent joke,
The absurdity. My burden
   Rolled off as I broke
Into laughter; and soon after
   I had found my own level;
With Balaam's Ass daily
   Out at grass I revel,
Now playing, now braying
   Over the meadows of light,
Our soaring, creaking Gloria,
   Our donkeys' delight.


## THE SMALL MAN
## ORDERS HIS WEDDING

With tambourines of amber, queens
In rose and lily garlanded
Shall go beside my noble bride
With dance and din and harmony,
And sabre clash and tabor crash
And lantern-light and torches flash
On shield and helmet, plume and sash,
The flower of all my armoury;

Till drawn at length by tawny strength
Of lions, lo! her chariot;
Their pride will brook no bridle – look,
No bit they bear, no farrier
Ere shod those feet that plod the street
Silent as ghosts; their savage heat
Is gentled as they draw my sweet,
New tamed herself, to marry me.

New swell from all the belfries tall,
Till towers reel, the revelry
Of iron tongue untiring swung
To booms and clangs of merriment!
While some prepare with trumpet blare
Before my gates to greet us there
When home we come; and everywhere
Let drum he rumbled steadily.

Once in, the roar and din no more
Are heard. The hot festivity
And blazing dies; from gazing eyes
These shadowy halls deliver her.
Yet neither flute nor blither lute
With pluck of amorous string be mute
Where happy maids their queen salute
And candle flames are quivering.

With decent stealth o'er fleecy wealth
Of carpets tripping soberly,
Depart each maid! Your part is played
And I to all her nobleness
Must mate my bare estate. How fair
The whole room has become! The air
Burns as with incense everywhere
Around, beneath, and over her.

What flame before our chamber door
Shines in on love's security?
Fiercer than day, its piercing ray
Pours round us unendurably.
It's Aphrodite's saffron light,
And Jove's monarchal presence bright
And Genius burning through the night
The torch of man's futurity.

For her the swords of furthest lords
Have flashed in fields ethereal;
The dynasts seven incline from heaven
With glad regard and serious,
And ponder there beyond our air
The infinite unborn, and care
For history, while the mortal pair
Lie drowned in dreaming weariness.


## THE COUNTRY OF THE BLIND

Hard light bathed them – a whole nation of eyeless men,
Dark bipeds not aware how they were maimed. A long
   Process, clearly, a slow curse,
      Drained through centuries, left them thus.

At some transitional stage, then, a luckless few
No doubt, must have had eyes after the up-to-date,
   Normal type had achieved snug
      Darkness, safe from the guns of heav'n;

Whose blind mouths would abuse words that belonged to their
Great-grandsires, unabashed, talking of light in some
   Eunuch'd, etiolated,
      Fungoid sense, as a symbol of

Abstract thoughts. If a man, one that had eyes, a poor
Misfit, spoke of the grey dawn or the stars or green-
   Sloped sea waves, or admired how
      Warm tints change in a lady's cheek,

None complained he had used words from an alien tongue,
None question'd. It was worse. All would agree. 'Of course,'

Came their answer. 'We've all felt
    Just like that.' They were wrong. And he

Knew too much to be clear, could not explain. The words –
Sold, raped, flung to the dogs – now could avail no more;
    Hence silence. But the mouldwarps,
        With glib confidence, easily

Showed how tricks of the phrase, sheer metaphors could set
Fools concocting a myth, taking the words for things.
    Do you think this a far-fetched
        Picture? Go then about among

Men now famous; attempt speech on the truths that once,
Opaque, carved in divine forms, irremovable,
    Dread but dear as a mountain-
        Mass, stood plain to the inward eye.


## ON BEING HUMAN

Angelic minds, they say, by simple intelligence
Behold the Forms of nature. They discern
Unerringly the Archtypes, all the verities
Which mortals lack or indirectly learn.
Transparent in primordial truth, unvarying,
Pure Earthness and right Stonehood from their clear,
High eminence are seen; unveiled, the seminal
                Huge Principles appear.

The Tree-ness of the tree they know – the meaning of
Arboreal life, how from earth's salty lap
The solar beam uplifts it, all the holiness
Enacted by leaves' fall and rising sap;

But never an angel knows the knife-edged severance
Of sun from shadow where the trees begin,
The blessed cool at every pore caressing us
      – An angel has no skin.

They see the Form of Air; but mortals breathing it
Drink the whole summer down into the breast.
The lavish pinks, the field new-mown, the ravishing
Sea-smells, the wood-fire smoke that whispers *Rest*.
The tremor on the rippled pool of memory
That from each smell in widening circles goes,
The pleasure and the pang – can angels measure it?
        An angel has no nose.

The nourishing of life, and how it flourishes
On death, and why, they utterly know; but not
The hill-born, earthy spring, the dark cold bilberries
The ripe peach from the southern wall still hot,
Full-bellied tankards foamy-topped, the delicate
Half-lyric lamb, a new loaf's billowy curves,
Nor porridge, not the tingling taste of oranges –
        An angel has no nerves.

Far richer they! I know the senses' witchery
Guards us, like air, from heavens too big to see;
Imminent death to man that barb'd sublimity
And dazzling edge of beauty unsheathed would be.
Yet here, within this tiny, charm'd interior,
This parlour of the brain, their Maker shares
With living men some secrets in a privacy
        Forever ours, not theirs.

# THE ECSTASY

Long had we crept in cryptic
Delights and doubts on tiptoes,
The air growing purer, clearer
Continually; and nearer
We went on to the centre of
The garden, hand in hand, finger on lip.

On right and left uplifted
The fountains rose with swifter
And steadier urgence, argent
On steely pillars, larger
Each moment, spreading foamy plumes
Thinner and broader under the blinding sun.

The air grows warmer; firmer
The silence grips it; murmur
Of insect buzz nor business
Of squirrel or bird there is not –
Only the fluttering of the butterflies
Above the empty lawns, dance without noise.

So on we fared and forded
A brook with lilies bordered,
So cold it wrung with anguish
Bitterly our hearts. But language
Cannot at all make manifest
The quiet centre we found on the other side.

Never such seal of silence
Did ice on streams or twilight
On birds impose. The pauses
In nature by her laws are

Imperfect; under the surface beats
A sound too constant to be ever observed.

From birth its stroke with equal
Dull rhythm, relentless sequence,
Taps on, unfelt, unaltered,
With beat that never falters –
Now known, like breathing, only when
It stopped. The permanent background failed our ear.

Said the voice of the garden, heard in
Our hearts, 'That was the burden
Of Time, his sombre drum-beat.
Here – oh hard to come by! –
True stillness dwells and will not change,
Never has changed, never begins nor ends.'

Who would not stay there, blither
Than memory knows? but either
Whisper of pride essayed us
Or meddling though betrayed us,
Then shuddering doubt – oh suddenly
We were outside, back in the wavering world.

## THE *SABOTEUSE*

Pity hides in the wood,
   The years and tides,
The earth, the bare moon,
   Death and birth,
The freezing skies, the sun
   And the populous seas
Against her, one and all,
   Are furiously incensed.

They have clashed spears to drown
   The noise of her tears;
They have whetted swords. Still
   They cannot forget.
Her faint noise in the wood
   Destroys all,
A soul-tormenting treason
   Threatening revolt.

They beat with clamorous gongs
   And din with hammers
To stun so light a noise
   They fear if once
Pity were heard aloud
   In the strong city,
Topless towers would fall,
   Engines stop.

Horribly alarmed, they have levied
   Their war and armed
All natural things against her.
   From horns and stings,
Mandibles, claws and paws

[52]

And the human hand,
From suns and ice, like a deer
    Pity runs;

Lest, if she wept in peace,
    While they slept,
(So they believe) the slow-
    Descending stream
Would grow to a pool, spread,
    Widen and overflow
And creep forth from the wood,
    Grown strong and deep.

And they would wake at morning
    And find a lake
Lapping against their walls,
    Mining, sapping,
Patiently eating away
    The strong foundations
Of the towers of pain, rising
    An inch in an hour;

Till the compassionate water
    Would ripple and plash
Far overhead, and the Powers
    Lay drowned and dead
Below, sharing the dark
    With shark and squid
And the forgotten shapes
    Of rotting wheels.

Therefore they woke destruction
    Against her and invoked
The Needs of the Sum of Things
    And the Coming Race
And the Claims of Order – oh all

The holiest names
Known in our hearts. They even
Included her own.


## THE LAST OF THE WINE

You think if we sigh, drinking the last decanter,
We're sensual topers, and thence you are ready to prose
And read your lecture. Need you? Why should you banter
Or badger us? Better imagine it thus; suppose

A man to have come from Atlantis eastward sailing –
Lemuria has fallen in the fury of a tidal wave,
The cities are drowned, the pitiless all-prevailing
Inhuman sea is Numinor's salt grave.

To Europe he comes from Lemuria, saved from the wreck
Of the gilded, loftily builded, countless fleet
With the violet sails. A phail hangs from his neck,
Holding the last of a golden cordial, subtle and sweet.

Unnamed is Europe, untamed; wet desolation
Of unwelcoming woods, the elk, the mammoth and the bear,
The fen and the forest. Men of a barbarous nation
On the sand in a circle standing await him there.

Horribly ridged are their foreheads. Weapons of bone,
Unhandy and blunt, they brandish in their clumsy grips.
Their females set up a screaming, their bagpipes drone;
They gaze and mumble. He raises the flask to his lips.

It brings to his mind the strings, the flutes, the tabors,
How he drank with poets at the banquet, robed and crowned,

He recalls the pillared halls carved with the labours
Of curious masters, (Lemuria's cities lie drowned),

The festal nights; the jest that flashed for a second
Light as a bubble, bright with a thousand years
Of nurture; the honour and virtue, the grace unreckoned
That sat like a robe on the Atlantean peers.

It has made him remember ladies, proud glances,
Fearless and peerless beauty, flower-like hair,
Ruses and mockery, the music of grave dances
(Where musicians played, huge fishes goggle and stare).

He sighs, like us; then rises and turns to meet
Those naked men. Will they make him their spoil and prey
Or salute him as god and brutally fawn at his feet?
And which would be worse? He pitches the phial away.

## AS ONE OLDSTER TO ANOTHER

Well, yes the bones ache. There were easier
Beds thirty years back. Sleep, then importunate,
    Now with reserve doles out her favours;
        Food disagrees; there are draughts in houses.

Headlong, the down night train rushes on with us,
Screams through the stations . . . how many more? Is it
    Time soon to think of taking down one's
        Case from the rack? Are we nearly there now?

Yet neither loss of friends, nor an emptying
Future, not England tamed and the ruin of
    Long-billed hopes thus far have taught my
        Obstinate heart a sedate deportment.

Still beauty calls as once in the mazes of
Boyhood. The bird-like soul quivers. Into her
    Flash darts of unfulfill'd desire and
        Pierce with a bright, unabated anguish.

Armed thus with anguish, joy met us even in
Youth – who forgets? This side of the terminus,
    Then, now, and always, thus, and only
        Thus, were the doors of delight set open.


## BALLADE OF DEAD GENTLEMEN

Where, in what bubbly land, below
    What rosy horizon dwells today
That worthy man Monsieur Cliquot
    Whose widow has made the world so gay?
    Where now is Mr Tanqueray?
Where might the King of Sheba be
    (Whose wife stopped dreadfully long away)?
*Mais où sont messieurs les maris?*

Say where did Mr Beeton go
    With rubicund nose and whiskers grey
To dream of dumplings long ago,
    Of syllabub soups, and *entremets*?
    In what dim isle did Twankey lay
His aching head? What murmuring sea
    Lulls him after the life-long fray?
*Mais où sont messieurs les maris?*

How Mr Grundy's cheeks may glow
    By a bathing-pool where lovelies play,
I guess, but shall I ever know?
    Where – if it comes to that, *who*, pray –

Is Mr Masham? Sévigné
And Mr Siddons and Zebedee
   And Gamp and Hemans, where are they?
*Mais où sont messieurs les maris?*

Princesses all, beneath your sway
   In this grave world they bowed the knee;
Libertine airs in Elysium say
   *Mais où sont messieurs les maris?*


## THE ADAM UNPARADISED

Faltering, with bowed heads, our altered parents
Slowly descended from their holy hill,
All their good fortune left behind and done with,
            Out through the one-way pass

Into the dangerous world, these strange countries.
No rumour in Eden had reached the human pair
Of things not men, yet half like men, that wandered
            The earth beyond its walls;

But now they heard the mountains stirred and shaken,
All the heap'd crags re-echoing, the deep tarns
And caverns shuddering and the abysmal gorges
            With dismal drums of Dwarfs;

Or, some prodigious night, waked by a thumping
Shock as of piles being driven two miles away,
Ran till the sunrise shone upon the bouncing
            Monopods at their heels;

Or held their breath, hiding, and saw their elders,
The race of giants – the bulldozer's pace,

Heads like balloons, toad-thick, ungainly torsos –
    Dotting the plain like ricks.

They had more to fear once Cain had killed a quarter
Of human kind and stolen away, and the womb
Of an unsmiling Hominid to the turncoat
    Had littered ominous sons.

A happy noise of liquid shapes, a lapping
Of small waves up and up the hills till all
Was smooth and silver, the clear Flood ascended
    Ending that crew; but still

Memory, not built upon a fake from Piltdown,
Reaches us. We know more than bones can teach.
Eve's body's language, Seth within her quickening,
    Taught him the sickening fear.

He passed the word. Before we're born we have heard it.
Long-silenced ogres boom, voices like gongs
Reverberate in the mind, a Dwarf-drum rolls,
    Trolls wind unchancy horns.

# THE ADAM AT NIGHT

Except at the making of Eve Adam slept
Not at all (as men now sleep) before the Fall;
Sin yet unborn, he was free from that dominion
Of the blind brother of death who occults the mind.

Instead, when stars and twilight had him to bed
And the dutiful owl, whirring over Eden, had hooted
A warning to the other beasts to be hushed till morning
And curbed their plays that the Man should be undisturbed,

He would lie, relaxed, enormous, under a sky
Starry as never since; he would set ajar
The door of his mind. Into him thoughts would pour
Other than day's. He rejoined Earth, his mother.

He melted into her nature. Gradually he felt
As though through his own flesh the elusive growth,
The hardening and spreading of roots in the deep garden;
In his veins, the wells filling with the silver rains,

And, thrusting down far under his rock-crust,
Finger-like, rays from the heavens that probed, bringing
To bloom the gold and diamond in his dark womb.
The seething, central fires moved with his breathing.

He guided his globe smoothly in the heaven, riding
At one with his planetary peers around the Sun;
Courteously he saluted the hard virtue of Mars
And Venus' liquid glory as he spun between them.

Over Man and his mate the Hours like waters ran
Till darkness thinned in the east. The treble lark,

Carolling, awoke the common people of Paradise
To yawn and scratch, to bleat and whinny, in the dawn.

Collected now in themselves, human and erect,
Lord and Lady walked on the dabbled sward,
As if two trees should arise dreadfully gifted
With speech and motion. The Earth's strength was in each.


# SOLOMON

Many a column of cedar was in Solomon's hall,
Much jade of China on the inlaid wall.
Cast aloft by the fountains with their soft foam,
A tremor of light was dancing in the emerald dome.

The popinjays on their perches without stopping praised
The unspeakable Name. The flamingoes and the peacocks blazed.
Incense richly darkened the day. Princes stood
Waiting – a motley diapason of robes hotly hued.

Like the column of a palm-tree, like a dolomite tower,
Like the unbearable noon-day in the glare of its power,
So solemn and so radiant was Solomon to behold,
Men feared his immense forehead and his beard of gold.

At his entry on the dais there went round
Flash of diamond, rustle of raiment, and a sighing sound
From among the ladies. They were wrung with desire,
Enslaving the heart. Musicians plucked the grave wire.

Like thunder at a distance came from under his feet
The rumble of captive Jinn and of humbled Efreet;
Column and foundation trembled; to Solomon's ring
Hell's abyss was obedient, and to the spells of the King.

By his bed lay crouching many a deadly Jinn;
He erected glory on their subjected sin,
By adamant will he was seeking the Adamite state,
The flame-like monarchy of Man. But he came late.

He was wrong. It was possible no longer. Among leaves
Bird-shaken, dew-scattering, it would have wakened Eve's
Maiden-cool laughter, could that lady have foretold
All his tragic apparatus – wives, magic, and gold.


## THE LATE PASSENGER

The sky was low, the sounding rain was falling dense and dark,
And Noah's sons were standing at the window of the Ark.

The beasts were in, but Japhet said, 'I see one creature more
Belated and unmated there come knocking at the door.'

'Well let him knock,' said Ham, 'Or let him drown or learn to swim.
We're overcrowded as it is; we've got no room for him.'

'And yet it knocks, how terribly it knocks,' said Shem, 'Its feet
Are hard as horn – but oh the air that comes from it is sweet.'

'Now hush,' said Ham, 'You'll waken Dad, and once he comes to see
What's at the door, it's sure to mean more work for you and me.'

Noah's voice came roaring from the darkness down below,
'Some animal is knocking. Take it in before we go.'

Ham shouted back, and savagely he nudged the other two,
'That's only Japhet knocking down a brad-nail in his shoe.'

Said Noah, 'Boys, I hear a noise that's like a horse's hoof.'
Said Ham, 'Why, that's the dreadful rain that drums upon the roof.'

Noah tumbled up on deck and out he put his head;
His face went grey, his knees were loosed, he tore his beard and said,

'Look, look! It would not wait. It turns away. It takes its flight.
Fine work you've made of it, my sons, between you all to-night!

'Even if I could outrun it now, it would not turn again
– Not now. Our great discourtesy has earned its high disdain.

'Oh noble and unmated beast, my sons were all unkind;
In such a night what stable and what manger will you find?

'Oh golden hoofs, oh cataracts of mane, oh nostrils wide
With indignation! Oh the neck wave-arched, the lovely pride!

'Oh long shall be the furrows ploughed across the hearts of men
Before it comes to stable and to manger once again,

'And dark and crooked all the ways in which our race shall walk,
And shrivelled all their manhood like a flower with broken stalk,

'And all the world, oh Ham, may curse the hour when you were born;
Because of you the Ark must sail without the Unicorn.'

# THE TURN OF THE TIDE

Breathless was the air over Bethlehem. Black and bare
    Were the fields; hard as granite the clods;
Hedges stiff with ice; the sedge in the vice
    Of the pool, like pointed iron rods.
And the deathly stillness spread from Bethlehem. It was shed
    Wider each moment on the land;
Through rampart and wall into camp and into hall
    Stole the hush; all tongues were at a stand.
At the Procurator's feast the jocular freedman ceased
    His story, and gaped. All were glum.
Travellers at their beer in a tavern turned to hear
    The landlord; their oracle was dumb.
But the silence flowed to the islands and the North
    And smoothed the unquiet river bars
And levelled out the waves from their revelling and paved
    The sea with cold reflected stars.
Where the Caesar on Palatine sat at ease to sign,
    Without anger, signatures of death,
There stole into his room and on his soul a gloom,
    And his pen faltered, and his breath.
Then to Carthage and the Gauls, past Parthia and the Falls
    Of Nile and Mount Amara it crept;
The romp and war of beast in swamp and jungle ceased,
    The forest grew still as though it slept.
So it ran about the girth of the planet. From the Earth
    A signal, a warning, went out
And away behind the air. Her neighbours were aware
    Of change. They were troubled with a doubt.


Salamanders in the Sun that brandish as they run
    Tails like the Americas in size

Were stunned by it and dazed; wondering, they gazed
      Up at Earth, misgiving in their eyes.
In houses and Signs Ousiarchs divine
      Grew pale and questioned what it meant;
Great Galactal lords stood back to back with swords
      Half-drawn, awaiting the event,
And a whisper among them passed, 'Is this perhaps the last
      Of our story and the glories of our crown?
– The entropy worked out? – The central redoubt
      Abandoned? The world-spring running down?'
Then they could speak no more. Weakness overbore
      Even them. They were as flies in a web,
In their lethargy stone-dumb. The death had almost come;
      The tide lay motionless at ebb.


Like a stab at that moment, over Crab and Bowman,
      Over Maiden and Lion, came the shock
Of returning life, the start and burning pang at heart,
      Setting Galaxies to tingle and rock;
And the Lords dared to breathe, and swords were sheathed
      And a rustling, a relaxing began,
With rumour and noise of the resuming of joys,
      On the nerves of the universe it ran.
Then pulsing into space with delicate, dulcet pace
      Came a music, infinitely small
And clear. But it swelled and drew nearer and held
      All worlds in the sharpness of its call.
And now divinely deep, and louder, with the sweep
      And quiver of inebriating sound,
The vibrant dithyramb shook Libra and the Ram,
      The brains of Aquarius spun round;
Such a note as neither Throne nor Potentate had known
      Since the Word first founded the abyss,
But this time it was changed in a mystery, estranged,
      A paradox, an ambiguous bliss.

Heaven danced to it and burned. Such answer was returned
　　　To the hush, the *Favete*, the fear
That Earth had sent out; revel, mirth and shout
　　　Descended to her, sphere below sphere.
Saturn laughed and lost his latter age's frost,
　　　His beard, Niagara-like, unfroze;
Monsters in the Sun rejoiced; the Inconstant One,
　　　The unwedded Moon, forgot her woes.
A shiver of re-birth and deliverance on the Earth
　　　Went gliding. Her bonds were released.
Into broken light a breeze rippled and woke the seas,
　　　In the forest it startled every beast.
Capripods fell to dance from Taproban to France,
　　　Leprechauns from Down to Labrador,
In his green Asian dell the Phoenix from his shell
　　　Burst forth and was the Phoenix once more.

So death lay in arrest. But at Bethlehem the bless'd
　　　Nothing greater could be heard
Than a dry wind in the thorn, the cry of the One new-born,
　　　And cattle in stall as they stirred.

# Part II

# THE BACKWARD GLANCE

# EVOLUTIONARY HYMN

Lead us, Evolution, lead us
   Up the future's endless stair:
Chop us, change us, prod us, weed us.
   For stagnation is despair:
Groping, guessing, yet progressing,
   Lead us nobody knows where.

Wrong or justice in the present,
   Joy or sorrow, what are they
While there's always jam to-morrow,
   While we tread the onward way?
Never knowing where we're going,
   We can never go astray.

To whatever variation
   Our posterity may turn
Hairy, squashy, or crustacean,
   Bulbous-eyed or square of stern,
Tusked or toothless, mild or ruthless,
   Towards that unknown god we yearn.

Ask not if it's god or devil,
   Brethren, lest your words imply
Static norms of good and evil
   (As in Plato) throned on high;
Such scholastic, inelastic,
   Abstract yardsticks we deny.

Far too long have sages vainly
   Glossed great Nature's simple text;
He who runs can read it plainly,
   'Goodness=what comes next.'

By evolving, Life is solving
    All the questions we perplexed.

Oh then! Value means survival –
    Value. If our progeny
Spreads and spawns and licks each rival,
    That will prove its deity
(Far from pleasant, by our present
    Standards, though it well may be).


## PRELUDE TO SPACE
*An Epithalamium*

So Man, grown vigorous now,
Holds himself ripe to breed,
Daily devises how
To ejaculate his seed
And boldly fertilize
The black womb of the unconsenting skies.

Some now alive expect
(I am told) to see the large,
Steel member grow erect,
Turgid with the fierce charge
Of our whole planet's skill,
Courage, wealth, knowledge, concentrated will;

Straining with lust to stamp
Our likeness on the abyss –
Bombs, gallows, Belsen camp,
Pox, polio, Thais' kiss
Or Judas', Moloch's fires
And Torquemada's (sons resemble sires).

Shall we, when the grim shape
Roars upward, dance and sing?
Yes: if we honour rape,
If we take pride to fling
So bountifully on space
The sperm of our long woes, our large disgrace.


## SCIENCE-FICTION
## CRADLESONG

By and by Man will try
To get out into the sky,
Sailing far beyond the air
From Down and Here to Up and There.
Stars and sky, sky and stars
Make us feel the prison bars.

Suppose it done. Now we ride
Closed in steel, up there, outside;
Through our port-holes see the vast
Heaven-scape go rushing past.
Shall we? All that meets the eye
Is sky and stars, stars and sky.

Points of light with black between
Hang like a painted scene
Motionless, no nearer there
Than on Earth, everywhere
Equidistant from our ship.
Heaven has given us the slip.

Hush, be still. Outer space
Is a concept, not a place.
Try no more. Where we are

Never can be sky or star.
From prison, in a prison, we fly;
There's no way into the sky.


## AN EXPOSTULATION
### *Against too many writers of science fiction*

Why did you lure us on like this,
Light-year on light-year, through the abyss,
Building (as though we cared for size!)
Empires that cover galaxies,
If at the journey's end we find
The same old stuff we left behind,
Well-worn Tellurian stories of
Crooks, spies, conspirators, or love,
Whose setting might as well have been
The Bronx, Montmartre, or Bethnal Green?

Why should I leave this green-floored cell,
Roofed with blue air, in which we dwell,
Unless, outside its guarded gates,
Long, long desired, the Unearthly waits,
Strangeness that moves us more than fear
Beauty that stabs with tingling spear,
Or Wonder, laying on one's heart
That finger-tip at which we start
As if some thought too swift and shy
For reason's grasp had just gone by?

## ODORA CANUM VIS
### *A defence of certain modern biographers and critics*

Come now, don't be too eager to condemn
Our little smut-hounds if they wag their tails
(Or shake like jellies as the tails wag them)
The moment the least whiff of sex assails
Their quivering snouts. Such conduct after all,
Though comic, is in them quite natural.

As those who have seen no lions must revere
A bull for Pan's *fortissimo*, or those
Who never tasted wine will value beer
Too highly, so the smut-hound, since he knows
Neither God, hunger, thought, nor battle, must
Of course hold disproportioned views on lust.

Of all the Invaders that's the only one
Even he could not escape; so have a heart,
Don't tie them up or whip them, let them run.
So! Cock your ears, my pretties! Play your part!
The dead are all before you, take your pick.
Fetch! Paid for! Slaver, snuff, defile and lick.

# ON A VULGAR ERROR

No. It's an impudent falsehood. Men did not
Invariably think the newer way
Porsaic, mad, inelegant, or what not.

Was the first pointed arch esteemed a blot
Upon the church? Did anybody say
How modern and how ugly? They did not.

Plate-armour, or windows glazed, or verse fire-hot
With rhymes from France, or spices from Cathay,
Were these at first a horror? They were not.

If, then, our present arts, laws, houses, food
All set us hankering after yesterday,
Need this be only an archaising mood?

Why, any man whose purse has been let blood
By sharpers, when he finds all drained away
Must compare how he stands with how he stood.

If a quack doctor's breezy ineptitude
Has cost me a leg, must I forget straightway
All that I can't do now, all that I could?

So, when our guides unanimously decry
The backward glance, I think we can guess why.

# THE FUTURE OF FORESTRY

How will the legend of the age of trees
Feel, when the last tree falls in England?
When the concrete spreads and the town conquers
The country's heart; when contraceptive
Tarmac's laid where farm has faded,
Tramline flows where slept a hamlet,
And shop-fronts, blazing without a stop from
Dover to Wrath, have glazed us over?
Simples tales will then bewilder
The questioning children, 'What was a chestnut?
Say what it means to climb a Beanstalk.
Tell me, grandfather, what an elm is.
What was Autumn? They never taught us.'
Then, told by teachers how once from mould
Came growing creatures of lower nature
Able to live and die, though neither
Beast nor man, and around them wreathing
Excellent clothing, breathing sunlight –
Half understanding, their ill-acquainted
Fancy will tint their wonder-paintings
–Trees as men walking, wood-romances
Of goblins stalking in silky green,
Of milk-sheen froth upon the lace of hawthorn's
Collar, pallor on the face of birchgirl.
So shall a homeless time, though dimly
Catch from afar (for soul is watchful)
A sight of tree-delighted Eden.

# LINES DURING A GENERAL ELECTION

Their threats are terrible enough, but we could bear
All that; it is their promises that bring despair.
If beauty, that anomaly, is left us still,
The cause lies in their poverty, not in their will.
If they had power ('amenities are bunk'), conceive
How their insatiate gadgetry by this would leave
No green, nor growth, nor quietude, no sap at all
In England from the Land's-End to the Roman Wall.
Think of their roads – broad as the road to Hell – by now
Murdering a million acres that demand the plough,
The thick-voiced Tannoy blaring over Arthur's grave,
And all our coasts one Camp till not the tiniest wave
Stole from the beach unburdened with its festal scum
Of cigarette-ends, orange-peel, and chewing-gum.
Nor would one island's rape suffice. Their visions are
Global; they mean the desecration of a Star;
Their happiest fancies dwell upon a time when Earth,
Flickering with sky-signs, gibbering with mechanic mirth,
One huge celestial charabanc, will stink and roll
Through patient heaven, subtopianized from pole to pole.

## THE CONDEMNED

There is a wildness still in England that will not feed
In cages; it shrinks away from the touch of the trainer's hand,
Easy to kill, not easy to tame. It will never breed
In a zoo for the public pleasure. It will not be planned.

Do not blame us too much if we that are hedgerow folk
Cannot swell the rejoicings at this new world you make
– We, hedge-hoggèd as Johnson or Borrow, strange to the yoke
As Landor, surly as Cobbett (that badger), birdlike as Blake.

A new scent troubles the air – to you, friendly perhaps –
But we with animal wisdom have understood that smell.
To all our kind its message is Guns, Ferrets, and Traps,
And a Ministry gassing the little holes in which we dwell.


## THE GENUINE ARTICLE

You do not love the Bourgeoisie. Of course: for they
Begot you, bore you, paid for you, and punched your head;
You work with them; they're intimate as board and bed;
How could you love them, meeting them thus every day?
You love the Proletariat, the thin, far-away
Abstraction which resembles any workman fed
On mortal food as closely as the shiny red
Chessknight resembles stallions when they stamp and neigh.

For kicks are dangerous; riding schools are painful, coarse
And ribald places. Every way it costs far less
To leave the harmless manage of the wooden horse

– So calculably taking the small jumps of chess.
Who, that can love nonentities, would choose the labour
Of loving the quotidian face and fact, his neighbour?


## ON THE ATOMIC BOMB
### Metrical Experiment


So; you have found an engine
Of injury that angels
Might dread. The world plunges,
Shies, snorts, and curvets like a horse in danger.

Then comfort her with fondlings,
With kindly word and handling,
But do not believe blindly
This way or that. Both fears and hopes are swindlers.

What's here to dread? For mortals
Both hurt and death were certain
Already; our light-hearted
Hopes from the first sentenced to final thwarting.

This marks no huge advance in
The dance of Death. His pincers
Were grim before with chances
Of cold, fire, suffocation, Ogpu, cancer.

Nor hope that this last blunder
Will end our woes by rending
Tellus herself asunder –
All gone in one bright flash like dryest tinder.,

As if your puny gadget
Could dodge the terrible logic

Of history! No; the tragic
Road will go on, new generations trudge it.

Narrow and long it stretches,
Wretched for one who marches
Eyes front. He never catches
A glimpse of the fields each side, the happy orchards.


## TO THE AUTHOR OF
### *FLOWERING RIFLE*

Rifles may flower and terrapins may flame
But truth and reason will be still the same.
Call them Humanitarians if you will,
The merciful are promised mercy still;
Loud fool! to think a nickname could abate
The blessing given to the compassionate.
Fashions in polysyllables may fright
Those Charlies on the Left of whom you write;
No wonder; since it was from them you learned
How white to black by jargon can be turned,
And though your verse outsoars with eagle pride
Their nerveless rhythms (of which the old cow died)
Yet your shrill covin-politics and theirs
Are two peas in a single pod – who cares
Which kind of shirt the murdering Party wears?
Repent! Recant! Some feet of sacred ground,
A target to both gangs, can yet be found,
Sacred because, though now it's no-man's land,
There stood your father's house; there you should stand.

# TO ROY CAMPBELL

Dear Roy – Why should each wowzer on the list
Of those you damn be dubbed Romanticist?
In England the romantic stream flows not
From waterish Rousseau but from manly Scott,
A right branch on the old European tree
Of valour, truth, freedom, and courtesy,
A man (though often slap-dash in his art)
Civilized to the centre of his heart,
A man who, old and cheated and in pain,
Instead of snivelling, got to work again,
Work without end and without joy, to save
His honour, and go solvent to the grave;
Yet even so, wrung from his failing powers,
One book of his would furnish ten of ours
With characters and scenes. The very play
Of mind, I think, is birth-controlled to-day.

It flows, I say, from Scott; from Coleridge too.
A bore? A sponge? A laudanum-addict? True;
Yet Newman in that ruinous master saw
One who restored our faculty for awe,
Who re-discovered the soul's depth and height,
Who pricked with needles of the eternal light
An England at that time half numbed to death
With Paley's, Bentham's, Malthus' wintry breath.
For this the reigning Leftist cell may be
His enemies, no doubt. But why should we?

Newman said much the same of Wordsworth too.
Now certain critics, far from dear to you,
May also fondle Wordsworth. But who cares?
Look at the facts. He's far more ours than theirs;
Or, if we carve him up, then all that's best
Falls to our share – we'll let them take the rest.

By rights the only half they should enjoy
Is the rude, raw, unlicked, North Country boy.


## CORONATION MARCH

Blow the trumpet! guardee tramp it!
Once to lord it thus was vulgar;
Then we could afford it; empire simpered,
Gold and gunboats were an ace of trumps.
Ranting poets then were plenty,
Loyalty meant royalties. Life is changing.
Now that bandogs mouth at random
Lion fallen into age and clawless,
Mid their snarling is the time for skirling
Pipes, and carefree scarlet. Therefore,
Rumble in the pageant drum-beat's magic,
Bunting wave on frontage bravely,
Grammar of heraldic rules unfolded
Spill forth gold and gules, and needling
Spire in floodlight pierce the midnight,
Pale as paper! Bright as any trumpet
Twinkle under taper gold of saintly
Crown of Edward; faintlier silver's
Elven gleam give female answer
With robe and globe and holiness of mitre.
Bray the trumpet, rumble tragic
Drum-beat's magic, sway the logic
Of legs that march a thousand in a uniform,
Flags and arches, the lion and the unicorn
Romp it, rampant, pompous tramping . . .
Some there are that talk of Alexander
    With a tow-row-row-row-row-row.

## 'MAN IS A LUMPE WHERE ALL
## BEASTS KNEADED BE'

Is this your duty? Never lay your ear
Back to your skull and snarl, bright Tiger! Down
Bruin! Grimalkin back! Did you not hear
        Man's voice and see Man's frown?

Too long, sleek purring Panther, you have paid
Your flatteries; far too long about my breast
You, Snake, like ivy have coiled. I'll not be stayed,
        I know my own way best.

Down, the whole pack! or else . . . so; now you are meek.
But then, alas, your eyes. Poor cowering brutes,
Your boundless pain, your strength to bear so weak –
        It bites at my heart-roots.

Oh, courage. I'll come back when I've grown shepherd
To feed you, and grown child to lead you all
Where there's green pasture waiting for the leopard
        And for the wolf a stall;

But not before I've come where I am bound
And made the end and the beginning meet,
When over and under Earth I have travelled round
        The whole heaven's milky street.

## ON A PICTURE BY CHIRICO

Two sovereign horses standing on the sand. There are no men,
The men have died, the houses fallen. A thousand years' war
Conclude in grass and graves and bones and waves on a bare shore
       Are rolled in a cold evening when there is rain in the air.

These were not killed and eaten with the rest. They were two swift
And strong for the last, stunted men to hunt in the great dearth.
Then they were already terrible. They inherit the large earth,
       The pleasant pastures, resonant with their snorting charge.

Now they have come to the end of land. They meet for the first time
In early, bitter March the falling arches of the sea, vast
And vacant in the sunset light, where once the ships passed.
       They halt, sniffing the salt in the air, and whinny with
         their lips.

These are not like the horses we have ridden; that old look
Of half-indignant melancholy and delicate alarm's gone.
Thus perhaps looked the breeding-pair in Eden when a day shone
       First upon tossing manes and glossy flanks at play.

They are called. Change overhangs them. Their neighing is half
         speech.
Death-sharp across great seas, a seminal breeze from the far side
Calls to their new-crowned race to leave the places where Man
         died –
       The offer, is it? the prophecy, of a Houyhnhnms' Land?

# ON A THEME
## FROM NICOLAS OF CUSA
### (De Docta Ignorantia, III.ix.)

When soul and body feed, one sees
Their differing physiologies.
Firmness of apple, fluted shape
Of celery, or tight-skinned grape
I grind and mangle when I eat,
Then in dark, salt, internal heat,
Annihilate their natures by
The very act that makes them I.

But when the soul partakes of good
Or truth, which are her savoury food,
By some far subtler chemistry
It is not they that change, but she,
Who feels them enter with the state
Of conquerors her opened gate,
Or, mirror-like, digests their ray
By turning luminous as they.

# WHAT THE BIRD SAID
## EARLY IN THE YEAR

I heard in Addison's Walk a bird sing clear
'This year the summer will come true. This year. This year.

'Winds will not strip the blossom from the apple trees
This year, nor want of rain destroy the peas.

'This year time's nature will no more defeat you,
Nor all the promised moments in their passing cheat you.

'This time they will not lead you round and back
To Autumn, one year older, by the well-worn track.

'This year, this year, as all these flowers foretell,
We shall escape the circle and undo the spell.

'Often deceived, yet open once again your heart,
Quick, quick, quick, quick! – the gates are drawn apart.'

# THE SALAMANDER

I stared into the fire; blue waves
Of shuddering heat that rose and fell,
And blazing ships and blinding caves,
Canyons and streets and hills of hell;
Then presently amidst it all
I saw a living creature crawl.

Forward it crept and pushed its snout
Between the bars, and with sad eyes
Into my quiet room looked out,
As men looked out upon the skies;
And from its scalding throat there came
A faint voice hissing like a flame:

'This is the end, the stratosphere,
The rim of the world where all life dies,
The vertigo of space, the fear
Of nothingness; before me lies
Blank silence, distances untold
Of unimaginable cold.

'Faint lights that fitfully appear
Far off in that immense abyss
Are but reflections cast from here,
There is no other fire but this,
This speck of life, this fading spark
Enisled amid the boundless dark.

'Blind Nature's measureless rebuke
To all we value, I received
Long since (though wishes bait the hook

With tales our ancestors believed)
And now can face with fearless eye
Negation's final sovereignty.'


## INFATUATION

Body and soul most fit for love can best
Withstand it. I am ill, and cannot rest,
Therefore I'm caught. Disease is amorous, health
At love's door has the pass both in and out.
Want cannot choose but grub with needy snout
In ravenous dreams, let temperance wait on wealth.
Don't think of her tonight . . . the very strain
Wears the will down; then in she comes by stealth.

How am I made that such a thing can trouble
My fancy for a day? Her brain's a bubble,
Her soul, a traveller's tale. Her every thrust
And trick I understand . . . the mould so mean,
And she the thousandth copy, comes between
My thoughts and me . . . unfrank, unfit for trust,
Yet ignorant in her cunning, a blind tool,
When nature bids her, labouring as she must.

Back to my book. Read. Read. Don't think upon her,
Where every thought is hatred and dishonour.
I do not love her, like her, wish her well.
Is it mere lust? But lust can quench his thirst
In any water; rather, at the first,
There was one moment when I could not tell
The thing she surely is. I stood unarmed
That moment, and the stroke that moment fell.

She stood, an image lost as soon as seen,
Like beauty in a vision half-caught between
Two aimless and long-lumbering dreams of night.
The thing I seek for was not anywhere
At any time on earth. That huntress air
And morning freshness was not hers by right.
She spoke, she smiled; put out what seemed the flame,
Left me the cold charred sticks, the ashes white.

And from these sprang the dream I dare not chase,
Lest, the long hunt being over, I embrace
My shadow. (Furies wait upon that bed)
It plucks me at the elbow . . . 'love can reach
That other soul of hers . . . charity teach
Atrophied powers once more to raise the head,
Sweet charity.' But she can never learn;
And what am I, whose voice should wake the dead?

How could she learn, who never since her birth
Looked out of her desires and saw the earth
Unshadowed by herself. She knows that man
Has whimsies, and will talk, and take concern
With wonderings and desires that serve no turn
Of woman. She would ape, (for well she can),
The rapt disciple at her need, till mask
Was needless . . . And all ends where it began.

Her holiest moods are gaudy desecrations
Of poor half holy things: her exaltations
Are frothed from music, moonlight, wine and dance;
Love is to her a dream of bridal dresses,
Friendship, a tittering hour of girl's caresses,
Virtue, a steady purpose to advance,
Honoured, and safe, by the old well-proven roads,
No loophole left to passion or to chance.

I longed last night to make her know the truth
That none of them has told her. Flushed with youth,
Dazed with a half-hour triumph, she held the crowd.
She loved the boys that buzzed on her like flies,
She loved the envy in the woman's eyes,
Faster she talked. I longed to cry aloud,
'What, has no brother told you yet, with whom
With what, you share the power that makes you proud?'

Could she have looked so noble, and no seed
Of spirit in her at all? But mother-greed
Has linked her boy-like splendour to the yoke.
Venus infernal taught such voice and eyes
To bear themselves abroad for merchandise . . .
Horrible woman-nature, at one stroke
Making the beauty, bending beauty down
To ruthless tasks, before the spirit awoke.

Thank heaven, though I were meshed and made secure,
Its odds, she'd never have me. I am poor . . .
Thank heaven, for if she did, what comes behind!
Can I not see her now, marked with my name,
Among my friends (shame not to hide my shame),
And her glib tongue runs on and rambles blind
Through slippery paths, revealing and revealing,
While they for my sake cover it and are kind.

Kind? Let them look at home. Which of them all
Knows how his act or word next hour may fall?
Into them, too, this might have come, unbidden,
Unlooked for. For each one of us, down below
The caldron brews in the dark. We do not know
By whom, or on what fields, we are reined and ridden.
There are not acts; spectators of ourselves
We wait and watch the event, the cause is hidden.

All power in man is mummery: good report
A fable: this apparent mind, the sport
For mumbling dynasts old as wind and tide.
Talk, posture, gild it over . . . still the motion
That moves us is not ours, but in the ocean
Of hunger and bleak fear, like buoys we ride,
And seem to move ourselves, and in the waves
Lifting and falling take our shame and pride.


## VOWELS AND SIRENS

Chosen to seduce you,
     Those dove-like vowels;
*Deuro – Kudos – Odusseus*
     Opening the bay, his prow

Appeared. Air rang with
     Siren voices;
The hero, bound, in anguish,
     Strove to retract his choice.

Nothing of solace
     For lovers' longings
They breathed. Of vanished knowledge
     Was their intemperate song,

A music that resembled
     Some earlier music
That men are born remembering.
     What all the gods refuse –

The backward journey
     To the steep river's

Hid source, the great returning –
      The Sirens feigned to give.

Cool voices, lying
      Words abuse us,
Cooing *Kudos Achaiôn*,
      Warbling their half-true news.


## THE PRUDENT JAILER

Always the old nostalgia? Yes.
We still remember times before
We had learned to wear the prison dress
Or steel rings rubbed our ankles sore.

Escapists? Yes. Looking at bars
And chains, we think of files; and then
Of black nights without moon or stars
And luck befriending hunted men.

Still when we hear the trains at night
We envy the free travellers, whirled
In how few moments past the sight
Of the blind wall that bounds our world.

Our Jailer (well he may) prefers
Our thoughts should keep a narrower range.
'The proper study of prisoners
Is prison,' he tells us. Is it strange?

And if old freedom in our glance
betrays itself, he calls it names
'Dope' – 'Wishful thinking' – or 'Romance',
Till tireless propaganda tames.

All but the strong whose hearts they break,
All but the few whose faith is whole.
Stone walls cannot a prison make
Half so secure as rigmarole.

## AUBADE

Eight strokes sound from within. The crowd, assembled
Outside, stare at the gate (it disregards them).
What lure brings them so early, under driving
Smoke-grey cloud with a hint of rain, before their
Day's work? Might pity draw them? Was the motive
Self-pleased – say, Pharisaical – delight in
Earth's old *lex talionis*? Easy answers,
Yet both short of the truth perhaps. The sharpest
Cause might be that amid the swirl of phantoms –
Film, broadcast, propaganda, picture-thinking –
Death, like cancer or crime or copulation,
Stands out real; and the soul with native hunger
(Called sensationalism in culture circles)
Seeks food ev'n in the dingiest of quarters.
I, snugged down in a bed, in warm refinement,
Dare not judge what attraction called and kept them,
Packed thus, waiting an hour or so to see the
Jail's black flag running up between the chimneys.

# PATTERN

Some believe the slumber
Of trees is in December
  When timber's naked under sky
And squirrel keeps his chamber.

But I believe their fibres
Awake to life and labour
  When turbulence comes roaring up
The land in loud October,

And plunders, strips, and sunders
And sends the leaves to wander
  And undisguises prickly shapes
Beneath the golden splendour.

Then form returns. In warmer,
Seductive days, disarming
  Its firmer will, the wood grew soft
And put forth dreams to murmur.

Into earnest winter
With spirit alert it enters;
  The hunter wind and the hound frost
Have quelled the green enchanter.

# AFTER ARISTOTLE

### 'Αρετα πολυμοχθε

Virtue, thou whom men with toil
Seek as their most precious spoil,
Gladly here in Greece for thy
Beauty, Virgin, men will die
And will live laborious days
And pass, unwearying, hard assays;
So arch-potent is thy touch
Upon mortal hearts, and such
Thy unfading fruit; by far
More esteemed than riches are;
Dearer than, and loved beyond
Our father kind, our mother fond;
Dearer even than the deep-
Dark eyes of the god of Sleep.

Swift as hounds in chase of thee
Leda's twin-born progeny
And Heracles, whom Zeus begot,
To their last hour fainted not;
Following through labours long
Thee who mak'st thy lovers strong;
So for thee Achilles and
Aias sought the silent land.

And now of late the nursling of
Atarneus town for thy dear love
Thought it not much to throw away
The sunlight of our mortal day.
Therefore all the daughters nine
Of Mnemosyne divine

Beyond the reach of death will raise
His name in song, nor from his praise
Disjoin the lauds of Zeus who best
Champions the truth of host to guest
And hallows the find cords that tie
Friendship indissolubly.


## REASON

Set on the soul's acropolis the reason stands
A virgin, arm'd, commercing with celestial light,
And he who sins against her has defiled his own
Virginity: no cleansing makes his garment white;
So clear is reason. But how dark, imagining,
Warm, dark, obscure and infinite, daughter of Night:
Dark is her brow, the beauty of her eyes with sleep
Is loaded, and her pains are long, and her delight.
Tempt not Athene. Wound not in her fertile pains
Demeter, nor rebel against her mother-right.
Oh who will reconcile in me both maid and mother,
Who make in me a concord of the depth and height?
Who make imagination's dim exploring touch
Ever report the same as intellectual sight?
Then could I truly say, and not deceive,
Then wholly, say, that I BELIEVE.

# TO ANDREW MARVELL

Marvell, they say your verse is faint
Beside the range of Donne's;
Too clear for them, too free from taint
Of noise, your music runs.

Their sultry minds can ill conceive
How godlike power should dwell
Except where lungs with torment heave
And giant muscles swell.

The better swordsman with a smile
His cool *passado* gives;
Smooth is the flooding of the Nile
By which all Egypt lives.

Sweetness and strength from regions far
Withdrawn and strange you bring,
And look no stronger than a star,
No graver than the spring.

# LINES WRITTEN IN A
## COPY OF MILTON'S WORKS

Alas! the happy beasts at pasture play
All, all alike; all of one mind are they;
By Nature with indifferent kindness blessed,
None loves a special friend beyond the rest;
No sparrow lacks a friend with whom to roam
All day for seeds till evening bids them home;
Whom if with cunning beak the cruel kite
Or peasant's arrow snatch from him tonight,
With a new friend next day, content, he wings his flight.
Not so is Man, who in his fellows finds
(Hard fate!) discordant souls and alien minds!
To him, though searching long, will scarce be shown
One heart amidst a thousand like his own;
Or if, at last relenting, fate shall send
In answer to his prayer, the authentic friend,
Him in some unsuspected hour, some day
He never dreaded, Death will snatch away
And leave behind a loss that time can ne'er allay.

Who now can charm to rest each eating care?
Who now the secrets of my bosom share?
Who now can while away with the delight
Of his discourse the livelong winter night,
When cracking nuts and hissing apples roast
Upon the hearth and from his southern coast
The wet wind in the elm-tree branches roars
And makes one vast confusion out of doors?

Alone I walk the fields and plains, alone
The dark vales with dense-branches overgrown.
Here, as day fades, I wait, and all around
I hear the rain that falls with sullen sound.

# SCHOLAR'S MELANCHOLY

The mind too has her fossils to record her past,
Cold characters, immobile, of what once was new
And hot with life. Old papers, as we rummage through
Neglected drawers, still show us where the pen, fast, fast,
Ate up the sheets: and wondering, we remember vast
Designs and knowledge gathered, and intent to do
What we were able then to have done . . . something drew
A sponge across that slate. The ferly would not last.

Though Will can stretch his viaduct with level thrust
High above shagg'd woods, quaking swamp, and desert dust
Of changing times, yet he must dig for his material
In local quarries of the varying moment – must
Use wattle and daub in countries without stone, and trust
To basest matter the proud arches' form imperial.

# Part III

# A LARGER WORLD

# WORMWOOD

Thou only art alternative to God, oh, dark
And burning island among spirits, tenth hierarch,
Wormwood, immortal Satan, Ahriman, alone
Second to Him to whom no second else were known,
Being essential fire, sprung of His fire, but bound
Within the lightless furnace of thy Self, bricked round
To rage in the reverberated heat from seven
Containing walls: hence power thou hast to rival heaven.
Therefore, except the temperance of the eternal love
Only thy absolute lust is worth thinking of.
All else is weak disguising of the wishful heart,
All that seemed earth is Hell, or Heaven. God is: thou art:
The rest, illusion. How should man live save as glass
To let the white light without flame, the Father, pass
Unstained: or else – opaque, molten to thy desire,
Venus infernal starving in the strength of fire!

Lord, open not too often my weak eyes to this.

# VIRTUE'S INDEPENDENCE

I have scraped clean the plateau from the filthy earth,
Earth the unchaste, the fruitful, the great grand maternal,
Sprawling creature, lolling at random and supine
The broad-faced, sluttish helot, the slave wife
Grubby and warm, who opens unashamed
Her thousand wombs unguarded to the lickerous sun.
Now I have scoured my rock clean from the filthy earth
On it no root can strike and no blade come to birth,
And though I starve of hunger it is plainly seen
That I have eaten nothing common or unclean.

I have by fasting purged away the filthy flesh,
Flesh the hot, moist, salt scum, the obscenity
And parasitic tetter, from my noble bones.
I have torn from my breasts – I was an udder'd beast –
My child, for he was fleshly. Flesh is caught
By a contagion carried from impure
Generation to generation through the body's sewer.
And now though I am barren, yet no man can doubt
I am clean and my iniquities are blotted out.

I have made my soul (once filthy) a hard, pure, bright
Mirror of steel: no damp breath breathes upon it
Warming and dimming it: it would freeze the finger
If any touched it. I have a mineral soul.
Minerals eat no food and void no excrement.
So I, borrowing nothing and repaying
Nothing, neither growing nor decaying,
Myself am to myself, a mortal God, a self-contained
Unwindowed monad, unindebted and unstained.

# POSTURING

Because of endless pride
Reborn with endless error,
Each hour I look aside
Upon my secret mirror
Trying all postures there
To make my image fair.

Thou givest grapes, and I,
Though starving, turn to see
How dark the cool globes lie
In the white hand of me,
And linger gazing thither
Till the live clusters wither.

So should I quickly die
Narcissus-like of want,
But, in the glass, my eye
Catches such forms as haunt
beyond nightmare, and make
Pride humble for pride's sake.

Then and then only turning
The stiff neck round, I grow
A molten man all burning
And look behind and know
Who made the glass, whose light makes
    dark, whose fair
Makes foul, my shadowy form reflected
    there
That self-love, brought to bed of Love
    may die and bear
Her sweet son in despair.

# DECEPTION

Iron will eat the world's old beauty up.
Girder and grid and gantry will arise,
Iron forest of engines will arise,
Criss-cross of iron crotchet. For your eyes
No green or growth. Over all, the skies
Scribbled from end to end with boasts and lies.
(When Adam ate the irrevocable apple, Thou
Saw'st beyond death the resurrection of the dead.)

Clamour shall clean put out the voice of wisdom,
The printing-presses with their clapping wings,
Fouling your nourishment. Harpy wings,
Filling your minds all day with foolish things,
Will tame the eagle Thought: till she sings
Parrot-like in her cage to please dark kings.
(When Israel descended into Egypt, Thou
Didst purpose both the bondage and the coming out.)

The new age, the new art, the new ethic and thought,
And fools crying, Because it has begun
It will continue as it has begun!
The wheel runs fast, therefore the wheel will run
Faster for ever. The old age is done,
We have new lights and see without the sun.
(Though they lay flat the mountains and dry up the sea,
Wilt thou yet change, as though God were a god?)

# DEADLY SINS

Through our lives thy meshes run
Deft as spiders' catenation,
Crossed and crossed again and spun
Finer than the fiend's temptation.

Greed into herself would turn
All that's sweet: but let her follow
Still that path, and greed will learn
How the whole world is hers to swallow.

Sloth that would find out a bed
Blind to morning, deaf to waking,
Shuffling shall at last be led
To the peace that knows no breaking.

Lechery, that feels sharp lust
Sharper from each promised staying,
Goes at long last – go she must –
Where alone is sure allaying

Anger, postulating still
Inexcusables to shatter,
From the shelter of thy will
Finds herself her proper matter.

Envy had rather die than see
Other's course her own outflying;
She will pay with death to be
Where her Best brooks no denying.

Pride, that from each step, anew
Mounts again with mad aspiring,

Must find all at last, save you,
Set too low for her desiring.

Avarice, while she finds an end,
Counts but small the largest treasure.
Whimperingly at last she'll bend
To take free what has no measure.

So inexorably thou
On thy shattered foes pursuing,
Never a respite dost allow
Save what works their own undoing.


## THE DRAGON SPEAKS

Once the worm-laid egg shattered in the wood.
I came forth shining into the trembling wood:
The sun was on my scales, dew upon the grasses,
The cold, sweet grasses and the sticky leaves.
I loved my speckled mate. We played at druery
And sucked warm milk dropping from the ewes' teats.

Now I keep watch on the gold in my rock cave
In a country of stones: old, deplorable dragon,
Watching my hoard. In winter night the gold
Freezes through tough scales my cold belly;
Jagged crowns, cruelly twisted rings,
Icy and knobb'd, are the old dragon's bed.

Often I wish I had not eaten my wife
(Though worm grows not to dragon till he eats worm).
She could have helped me, watch and watch about,
Guarding the gold; the gold would have been safer.
I could uncoil my tired body and take
Sometimes a little sleep when she was watching.

Last night under the moonset a fox barked,
Startled me; then I knew I had been sleeping.
Often an owl flying over the country of stones
Startles me; then I think that I must have slept,
Only a moment. That very moment a Man
might have come from the towns to steal my gold.

They make plots in the towns to take my gold,
They whisper of me in the houses, making plans,
Merciless men. Have they not ale upon the benches,
Warm wives in bed, and song, and sleep the whole night?
I leave my cave once only in the winter
To drink at the rock pool; in summer twice.

They have no pity for the old, lugubrious dragon.
Lord that made the dragon, grant me thy peace,
But say not that I should give up the gold,
Nor move, nor die. Others would have the gold.
Kill rather, Lord, the Men and the other dragons;
Then I can sleep; go when I will to drink.

# DRAGON-SLAYER

I have come back with victory got –
But stand away – touch me not
Even with your clothes. I burn red-hot.

The worm was bitter. When she saw
My shield glitter beside the shaw
She spat flame from her golden jaw.

When on my sword her vomit spilt
The blade took fire. On the hilt
Beryl cracked, and bubbled gilt.

When sword and sword arm were all flame
With the very heat that came
Out of the brute, I flogged her tame.

In her own spew the worm died.
I rolled her round and tore her wide
And plucked the heart from her boiling side.

When my teeth were in the heart
I felt a pulse within me start
As though my breast would break apart.

It shook the hills and made them reel
And spun the woods round like a wheel.
The grass singed where I set my heel.

Behemoth is my serving man!
Before the conquered hosts of Pan
Riding tamed Leviathan,
Loud I sing for well I can
*RESVRGAM* and *Io PAEAN*,
*Io, Io, Io, PAEAN!*

Now I know the stake I played for,
Now I know what a worm's made for!


## LILITH

When Lilith means to draw me
Within her secret bower,
She does not overawe me
With beauty's pomp and power,
Nor, with angelic grace
Of courtesy, and the pace
Of gliding ships, comes veiled at evening hour.

Eager, unmasked, she lingers
Heart-sick and hunger sore;
With hot, dry, jewelled fingers
Stretched out, beside her door,
Offering with gnawing haste
Her cup, whereof who taste,
(She promises not better) thirst far more.

What moves me, then, to drink it?
– Her spells, which all around
So change the land, we think it
A great waste where a sound
Of wind like tales twice told
Blusters, and cloud is rolled
Always above yet no rain falls to ground.

Across drab iteration
Of bare hills, line on line,
The long road's sinuation
Leads on. The witch's wine,
Though promising nothing, seems
In that land of no streams,
To promise best – the unrelished anodyne.

# A PAGEANT PLAYED IN VAIN

Watching the thought that moves
Within my conscient brain,
I learn how often that appearance proves
A pageant played in vain.

Holding what seems the helm,
I make a show to steer,
But winds, for worse and better, overwhelm
My purpose, and I veer.

Thus, if thy guidance reach
Only my head, then all
Hardest attempt of mine serves but to teach
How oddly the dice fall.

To limbs, and loins, and heart,
Search with thy chemic beam,
Strike where the self I know not lives apart,
Beneath the surface dream.

break, Sun, my crusted earth,
Pierce, razor-edged, within,
Where blind, immortal metals have their birth,
And crystals clear begin.

Thy spirit in secret flows
About our lives. In gloom,
The mother helping not nor hindering, grows
The child within the womb.

# WHEN THE CURTAIN'S DOWN

I am not one that easily flits past in thought
The ominous stream, imagining death made for nought.
This person, mixed of body and breath, to which concurred
Once only one articulation of thy word,
Will be resolved eternally: nor can time bring
(Else time were vain) once back again the self-same thing.
Therefore among the riddles that no man has read
I put thy paradox, Who liveth and was dead.
As Thou hast made substantially, Thou wilt unmake
In earnest and for everlasting. Let none take
Comfort in frail supposal that some hour and place
To those who mourn recovers the wished voice and face.
Whom Thy great *Exit* banishes, no after age
Of epilogue leads back upon the lighted stage.
Where is Prince Hamlet when the curtain's down? Where fled
Dreams at the dawn, or colours when the light is sped?
We are thy colours, fugitive, never restored,
Never repeated again. Thou only art the Lord,
Thou only art holy. In the shadowy vast
Of thine Osirian wings Thou dost enfold the past.
There sit in throne antediluvian, cruel kings,
There the first nightingale that sang to Eve yet sings,
There are the irrecoverable guiltless years,
There, yet unfallen, Lucifer among his peers.

For thou art also a deity of the dead, a god
Of graves, with necromancies in thy potent rod;
Thou art Lord of the unbreathable transmortal air
Where mortal thinking fails: night's nuptial darkness, where
All lost embraces intermingle and are bless'd,
And all die, but all are, while Thou continuest.

# DIVINE JUSTICE

God in His mercy made
The fixed pains of Hell.
That misery might be stayed,
God in His mercy made
Eternal bounds and bade
Its waves no further swell.
God in His mercy made
The fixed pains of Hell


# EDEN'S COURTESY

Such natural love twixt beast and man we find
That children all desire an animal book,
And all brutes, not perverted from their kind,
Woo us with whinny, tongue, tail, song, or look;
    So much of Eden's courtesy yet remains.
But when a creature's dread, or mine, has built
A wall between, I think I feel the pains
That Adam earned and do confess my guilt.
    For till I tame sly fox and timorous hare
And lording lion in my self, no peace
Can be without; but after, I shall dare
Uncage the shadowy zoo and war will cease;
    Because the brutes within, I do not doubt,
Are archetypal of the brutes without.

# THE METEORITE

Among the hills a meteorite
Lies huge; and moss has overgrown,
And wind and rain with touches light
Made soft, the contours of the stone.

Thus easily can Earth digest
A cinder of sidereal fire,
And make the translunary guest
Thus native to an English shire.

Nor is it strange these wanderers
Find in her lap their fitting place,
For every particle that's hers
Came at the first from outer space.

All that is Earth has once been sky;
Down from the Sun of old she came,
Or from some star that travelled by
Too close to his entangling flame.

Hence, if belated drops yet fall
From heaven, on these her plastic power
Still works as once it worked on all
The glad rush of the golden shower.

# TWO KINDS OF MEMORY

Oh still vacation, silver
Pause and relaxing of severer laws,
Oh Memory the compassionate,
Forever in dim labyrinths of reverie
The cruel past disarming and refashioning!

But iron Memory, tyrant
Importunate by night, with lucid torture
Still back into the merciless
Unalterable fact, the choking halter of
The finished past, where nothing grows, coercing us!

Well did our brooding elders
Appoint both king and queen, two powers with joint
Authority in the underworld;
Persephone, the lost and found, the ineffable
Daughter of the buried spring, the wise, the wonderful;

But made her consort Hades
Stern and exact, whom no one's prayer can turn
Nor length of years can mitigate.
On Orpheus when, the second time, he forfeited
Eurydice, he gazed, correct and pitiless.

His Mercies ev'n are cursèd
Mockeries of life, cold, cold as lunar rock,
And all his famed Elysium
Worthless, if former joys in all their earthliness
Are there repeated, manically, dizzily,

And round forever, bound for
No goal, upon a circling track, the soul

Re-lives her past; – Orion on
His quarry, and upon his foe the warrior,
Ever pursuing or forever triumphing.

In her the heaviest burthen
Grows light; old shame or sorrow or heart-blight
Seen in her glass turn magical;
A splendour, a rich gloom, a dewy tenderness
Silently overgrows the graves of tragedy.

And joys remembered, poising
A moment on the past which was their home,
Soon without longer tarrying
Take flight and never rest until they light upon
The branches of the deep-leaved woods of Paradise.

Who calls such magic falsehood
Must swear the mummy tells of the dead Pharaoh
More truth than all the merriment
And gold of all the harvests ever told us of
The seed that yearly breaks from yearly burial.

# RE-ADJUSTMENT

I thought there would be a grave beauty, a sunset splendour
In being the last of one's kind: a topmost moment as one watched
The huge wave curving over Atlantis, the shrouded barge
Turning away with wounded Arthur, or Ilium burning.
Now I see that, all along, I was assuming a posterity
Of gentle hearts: someone, however distant in the depths of time,
Who could pick up our signal, who could understand a story. There
    won't be.
Between the new *Hominidae* and us who are dying, already
There rises a barrier across which no voice can ever carry,
For devils are unmaking language. We must let that alone forever.
Uproot your loves, one by one, with care, from the future,
And trusting to no future, receive the massive thrust
And surge of the many-dimensional timeless rays converging
On this small, significant dew drop, the present that mirrors all.


# NEARLY THEY STOOD

Nearly they stood who fall.
Themselves, when they look back,
See always in the track
One torturing spot where all
By a possible quick swerve
Of will yet unenslaved –
By the infinitesimal twitching of a nerve –
Might have been saved.

Nearly they fell who stand.
These with cold after-fear
Look back and note how near
They grazed the Siren's land,

Wondering to think that fate,
By threads so spidery-fine,
The choice of ways so small, the event so great,
Should thus entwine.

Therefore I sometimes fear
Lest oldest fears prove true,
Lest, when no bugle blew
My mort, when skies looked clear,
I may have stepped one hair's
Breadth past the hair-breadth bourn
Which, being once crossed forever unawares,
Forbids return.


RELAPSE

Out of the wound we pluck
The shrapnel. Thorns we squeeze
Out of the hand. Even poison forth we suck,
And after pain have ease.

But images that grow
Within the soul have life
Like cancer and, often cut, live on below
The deepest of the knife,

Waiting their time to shoot
At some defenceless hour
Their poison, unimpaired, at the heart's root,
And, like a golden shower,

Unanswerably sweet,
Bright with returning guilt,

Fatally in a moment's time defeat
Our brazen towers long-built;

And all our former pain
And all our surgeon's care
Is lost, and all the unbearable (in vain
Borne once) is still to bear.


## LATE SUMMER

I, dust and bedraggled as I am,
Pestered with wasps and weeds and making jam,
Blowzy and stale, my welcome long outstayed,
Proved false in every promise that I made,
At my beginning I believed, like you,
Something would come of all my green and blue.
Mortals remember, looking on the thing
I am, that I, even I, was once a spring.


## TO A FRIEND

If knowledge like the mid-day heat
Uncooled with cloud, unstirred with breath
Of undulant air, begins to beat
On minds one moment after death,

From your rich soil what lives will spring,
What flower-entangled paradise,
Through what green walks the birds will sing,
What med'cinable gums, what spice,

Apples of what smooth gold! But fear
Gnaws at me for myself; the noon
That nourishes Earth can only sear
And scald the unresponding Moon.

Her gaping valleys have no soil,
Her needle-pointed hills are bare;
Water, poured on those rocks, would boil,
And day lasts long, and long despair.


## TO CHARLES WILLIAMS

Your death blows a strange bugle call, friend, and all is hard
To see plainly or record truly. The new light imposes change,
Re-adjusts all a life-landscape as it thrusts down its probe from the
    sky,
To create shadows, to reveal waters, to erect hills and deepen glens.
The slant alters. I can't see the old contours. It's a larger world
Than I once thought it. I wince, caught in the bleak air that blows
    on the ridge.
Is it the first sting of the great winter, the world-waning? Or the
    cold of spring?

A hard question and worth talking a whole night on. But with
    whom?
Of whom now can I ask guidance? With what friend concerning
    your death
Is it worth while to exchange thoughts unless – oh unless it were
    you?

# AFTER VAIN PRETENCE

When the grape of the night is pressed
Nearly dry, and the trains rest
And roads are empty and the moon low,
out of my body's breast I go,
Insecure, as a child escaped,
Animula flittering in the night unshaped;
Lacking wings; but I leap so high
It wants but a little more to fly.
Down I swoop with a seven-league stride
From church's spire to river side,
There scarce touching the ground, and then
Up to the elm-tree tops again;
Rising higher each leap and still
Sinking lower again, until
Lured to venture at last too much
I dream of flying indeed – no touch
Of earth between; then, holding breath
I poise on a perilous edge. But faith
All goes out of my soul – too late!
Air is emptiness: man has weight.
Unsupported I drop like lead
To where my body awakes in bed
Screaming-scared – and yet glad, as one
Who, after vain pretence, has done
With keeping company too great
For his lean purse and low estate.

# ANGEL'S SONG

I know not, I,
   What the men together say,
How lovers, lovers die
   And youth passes away.

Cannot understand
   Love that mortal bears
To native, native land,
   All lands are theirs;

Why at grave they grieve
   For one voice and face,
And not, and not receive
   Another in its place.

I above the cone
   Of the circling night
Flying, never have known
   Less or greater light.

Sorrow it is they call
   This cup whence my lip
(Woe's me!) never in all
   My endless days can sip.

# JOYS THAT STING

*Oh doe not die*, says Donne, *for I shall hate*
*All women so.* How false the sentence rings.
Women? But in a life made desolate
It is the joys once shared that have the stings.

To take the old walks alone, or not at all,
To order one pint where I ordered two,
To think of, and then not to make, the small
Time-honoured joke (senseless to all but you);

To laugh (oh, one'll laugh), to talk upon
Themes that we talked upon when you were there,
To make some poor pretence of going on,
Be kind to one's old friends, and seem to care,

While no one (O God) through the years will say
The simplest, common word in just your way.

## OLD POETS REMEMBERED

One happier look on your kind, suffering face,
And all my sky is domed with cloudless blue;
Eternal summer in a moment's space
Breathes with sweet air and glows and warms me through.

One droop of your dear mouth, one tear of yours,
One gasp of Faith half-strangled by its foe,
And down through a waste world of slag and sewers
And hammering and loud wheels once more I go.

Thus, what old poets told me about love
(Tristram's obedience, Isoud's sovereignty . . .)
Turns true in a dread mode I dreamed not of,
– What once I studied, now I learn to be;

Taught, oh how late! in anguish, the response
I might have made with exultation once.


## AS THE RUIN FALLS

All this is flashy rhetoric about loving you.
I never had a selfless thought since I was born.
I am mercenary and self-seeking through and through:
I want God, you, all friends, merely to serve my turn.

Peace, re-assurance, pleasure, are the goals I seek,
I cannot crawl one inch outside my proper skin:
I talk of love – a scholar's parrot may talk Greek –
But, self-imprisoned, always end where I begin.

Only that now you have taught me (but how late) my lack.
I see the chasm. And everything you are was making
My heart into a bridge by which I might get back
From exile, and grow man. And now the bridge is breaking.

For this I bless you as the ruin falls. The pains
You give me are more precious than all other gains.

# Part IV

# NOON'S INTENSITY

## POEM FOR PSYCHOANALYSTS
## AND/OR THEOLOGIANS

Naked apples, woolly-coated peaches
Swelled on the garden's wall. Unbounded
Odour of windless, spice-bearing trees
Surrounded my lying in sacred turf,
Made dense the guarded air – the forest of trees
Buoyed up therein like weeds in ocean
Lived without motion. I was the pearl,
Mother-of-pearl my bower. Milk-white the cirrhus
Streaked the blue egg-shell of the distant sky,
Early and distant, over the spicy forest;
Wise was the fangless serpent, drowsy.
All this, indeed, I do not remember.
I remember the remembering, when first waking
I heard the golden gates behind me
Fall to, shut fast. On the flinty road,
Black-frosty, blown on with an eastern wind,
I found my feet. Forth on journey,
Gathering thin garment over aching bones,
I went. I wander still. But the world is round.

## NOON'S INTENSITY

Till your alchemic beams turn all to gold
There must be many metals. From the night
You will not yet withdraw her silver light,
And often with Saturnian tints the cold
Atlantic swells at morning shall enfold
The Cornish cliffs burnished with copper bright;
Till trained by slow degrees we have such sight
As dares the pure projection to behold.
Even when Sol comes ascendant, it may be
More perfectly in him our eyes shall see
All baser virtues; thus shall hear you talking
And yet not die. Till then, you have left free,
Unscorched by your own noon's intensity
One cool and evening hour for garden walking.

## SWEET DESIRE

These faint wavering far-travell'd gleams
Coming from your country, fill me with care. That scent,
That sweet stabbing, as at the song of thrush,
That leap of the heart – too like they seem
To another air; unlike as well
So that I am dazed with doubt. As a dungeoned man
Who has heard the hinge on the hook turning
Often. Always that opened door
Let new tormentors in. If now at last
It opened again, but outward, offering free way,
(His Kind one come, with comfort) he
Yet shrinks, in his straw, struggling backward,

From his dear, from his door, into the dark'st corner,
Furthest from freedom. So, fearing, I
Taste not but with trembling. I was tricked before.
All the heraldry of heaven, holy monsters,
With hazardous and dim half-likeness taunt
Long-haunted men. The like is not the same.
Always evil was an ape. I know.
Who passes to paradise, within that pure border
Finds there, refashioned, all that he fled from here.
And yet . . .
            But what's the use? For yield I must,
Though long delayed, at last must dare
To give over, to be eased of my iron casing,
Molten at thy melody, as men of snow
In the solar smile. Slow-paced I come,
Yielding by inches. And yet, oh Lord, and yet,
– Oh Lord, let not likeness fool me again.


## CAUGHT

You rest upon me all my days
The inevitable Eye,
Dreadful and undeflected as the blaze
Of some Arabian sky;

Where, dead still, in their smothering tent
Pale travellers crouch, and, bright
About them, noon's long-drawn Astonishment
Hammers the rocks with light.

Oh, for but one cool breath in seven,
One air from northern climes,
The changing and the castle-clouded heaven
Of my old Pagan times!

But you have seized all in your rage
Of Oneness. Round about,
Beating my wings, all ways, within your cage,
I flutter, but not out.

## FORBIDDEN PLEASURE

Quick! The black, sulphurous, never quenched,
Old festering fire begins to play
Once more within. Look! By brute force I have wrenched
Unmercifully my hands the other way.

Quick, Lord! On the rack thus, stretched tight,
Nerves clamouring as at nature's wrong.
Scorched to the quick, whipp'd raw – Lord, in this plight
You see, you see no man can suffer long.

Quick, Lord! Before new scorpions bring
New venom – ere fiends blow the fire
A second time – quick, show me that sweet thing
Which, 'spite of all, more deeply I desire.

# THE NAKED SEED

My heart is empty. All the fountains that should run
      With longing, are in me
Dried up. In all my countryside there is not one
      That drips to find the sea.
I have no care for anything thy love can grant
      Except the moment's vain
And hardly noticed filling of the moment's want
      and to be free from pain.
Oh, thou that art unwearying, that dost neither sleep
      Nor slumber, who didst take
All care for Lazarus in the careless tomb, oh keep
      Watch for me till I wake.
If thou think for me what I cannot think, if thou
      Desire for me what I
Cannot desire, my soul's interior Form, though now
      Deep-buried, will not die,
– No more than the insensible dropp'd seed which grows
      Through winter ripe for birth
Because, while it forgets, the heaven remembering throws
      Sweet influence still on earth,
– Because the heaven, moved moth-like by thy beauty, goes
      Still turning round the earth.

# SCAZONS

Walking to-day by a cottage I shed tears
When I remembered how once I had walked there
With my friends who are mortal and dead. Years
Little had healed the wound that was laid bare.

Out little spear that stabs! I, fool, believed
I had outgrown the local, unique sting,
I had transmuted wholly (I was deceived)
Into Love universal the lov'd thing.

But Thou, Lord, surely knewest thine own plan
When the angelic indifferencies with no bar
Universally loved, but Thou gav'st man
The tether and pang of the particular,

Which, like a chemic drop, infinitesimal,
Plashed into pure water, changing the whole,
Embodies and embitters and turns all
Spirit's sweet water into astringent soul,

That we, though small, might quiver with fire's same
Substantial form as Thou – not reflect merely
Like lunar angels back to Thee cold flame.
Gods are we, Thou hast said; and we pay dearly.

# LEGION

Lord, hear my voice, my present voice I mean,
Not that which may be speaking an hour hence
(For I am Legion) in an opposite sense,
And not by show of hands decide between
The multiple factions which my state has seen
Or will see. Condescend to the pretence
That what speaks now is I; in its defence
Dissolve my parliament and intervene.

Thou wilt not, though we asked it, quite recall
Free will once given. Yet to this moment's choice
Give unfair weight. Hold me to this. Oh strain
A point – use legal fictions; for if all
My quarrelling selves must bear an equal voice,
Farewell, thou has created me in vain.


# PILGRIM'S PROBLEM

By now I should be entering on the supreme stage
Of the whole walk, reserved for the late afternoon.
The heat was to be over now; the anxious mountains,
The airless valleys and the sun-baked rocks, behind me.

Now, or soon now, if all is well, come the majestic
Rivers of foamless charity that glide beneath
Forests of contemplation. In the grassy clearings
Humility with liquid eyes and damp, cool nose
Should come, half-tame, to eat bread from my hermit hand.
If storms arose, then in my tower of fortitude –

It ought to have been in sight by this – I would take refuge;
But I expected rather a pale mackerel sky,
Feather-like, perhaps shaking from a lower cloud
Light drops of silver temperance, and clovery earth
Sending up mists of chastity, a country smell,
Till earnest stars blaze out in the established sky
Rigid with justice; the streams audible; my rest secure.

I can see nothing like all this. Was the map wrong?
Maps can be wrong. But the experienced walker knows
That the other explanation is more often true.


## SONNET

*Dieu a établi la prière pour communiquer à ses
creatures la dignité de la causalité* – PASCAL

The Bible says Sennacherib's campaign was spoiled
By angels: in Herodotus it says, by mice –
Innumerably nibbling all one night they toiled
To eat his bowstrings piecemeal as warm wind eats ice.

But muscular archangels, I suggest, employed
Seven little jaws at labour on each slender string,
And by their aid, weak masters though they be, destroyed
The smiling-lipped Assyrian, cruel-bearded king.

No stranger that omnipotence should choose to need
Small helps than great – no stranger if His action lingers
Till men have prayed, and suffers their weak prayers indeed
To move as very muscles His delaying fingers,

Who, in His longanimity and love for our
Small dignities, enfeebles, for a time, His power.

[134]

# THE PHOENIX

The Phoenix flew into my garden and stood perched upon
    A sycamore; the feathered flame with dazzling eyes
Lit up the whole lawn like a bonfire on midsummer's eve.
    I ran out, slipping on the grass, reeling beneath
The news I bore: 'The Sole Bird is not fabulous! Look! Look!'
    The dark girl, passing in the road, heard me. Her eyes
Lit up (I saw her features flood-lit in those golden rays)
    So that I called, or else the Bird called, and we went
Over the wet lawn – shadows for our train – towards the Wonder.
    Then, looking round, I saw her eyes . . . could it be true?
Was I deceived? . . . oh, say I was deceived . . . I thought her eyes
    Had all along been fixed on me, not on the Bird.

Thrice-honoured Lady, make not of your spoon your meat, for silver
(How much less, tin or wood?) contains no nourishment.
I will be all things, any thing, to you, save only that.
    Break not our hearts by telling me you never saw
The Phoenix, that my trumpery silhouette, thrusting between,
    Made an eclipse. For I had dreamed that I had caught
For his own beak a silver, shining fish such as he loves,
    And, having little of my own to offer Him,
Was building much on this miraculous draught. If the line breaks,
    Oh with what empty hands you send me back to Him!

# THE NATIVITY

Among the oxen (like an ox I'm slow)
I see a glory in the stable grow
Which, with the ox's dullness might at length
        Give me an ox's strength.

Among the asses (stubborn I as they)
I see my Saviour where I looked for hay;
So may my beastlike folly learn at least
        The patience of a beast.

Among the sheep (I like a sheep have strayed)
I watch the manger where my Lord is laid;
Oh that my baa-ing nature would win thence
        Some woolly innocence!

# PRAYER

Master, they say that when I seem
   To be in speech with you,
Since you make no replies, it's all a dream
   – One talker aping two.

They are half right, but not as they
   Imagine; rather, I
Seek in myself the things I meant to say,
   And lo! the wells are dry.

Then, seeing me empty, you forsake
   The Listener's rôle, and through
My dead lips breathe and into utterance wake
   The thoughts I never knew.

[136]

And thus you neither need reply
  Nor can; thus, while we seem
Two talking, thou art One forever, and I
  No dreamer, but thy dream.


## LOVE'S AS WARM
## AS TEARS

Love's as warm as tears,
  Love is tears:
Pressure within the brain,
Tension at the throat,
Deluge, weeks of rain,
Haystacks afloat,
Featureless seas between
Hedges, where once was green.

Love's as fierce as fire,
  Love is fire:
All sorts – infernal heat
Clinkered with greed and pride,
Lyric desire, sharp-sweet,
Laughing, even when denied,
And that empyreal flame
Whence all loves came.

Love's as fresh as spring,
  Love is spring:
Bird-song hung in the air,
Cool smells in a wood,
Whispering 'Dare! Dare!'
To sap, to blood,
Telling 'Ease, safety, rest,
  Are good; not best.'

Love's as hard as nails,
    Love is nails:
Blunt, thick, hammered through
The medial nerves of One
Who, having made us, knew
The thing He had done,
Seeing (with all that is)
Our cross, and His.


## NO BEAUTY WE COULD DESIRE

Yes, you are always everywhere. But I,
Hunting in such immeasurable forests,
Could never bring the noble Hart to bay.

The scent was too perplexing for my hounds;
Nowhere sometimes, then again everywhere.
Other scents, too, seemed to them almost the same.

Therefore I turn my back on the unapproachable
Stars and horizons and all musical sounds,
Poetry itself, and the winding stair of thought.

Leaving the forests where you are pursued in vain
– Often a mere white gleam – I turn instead
To the appointed place where you pursue.

Not in Nature, not even in Man, but in one
Particular Man, with a date, so tall, weighing
So much, talking Aramaic, having learned a trade;

Not in all food, not in all bread and wine
(Not, I mean, as my littleness requires)
But this wine, this bread . . . no beauty we could desire.

## STEPHEN TO LAZARUS

But was I the first martyr, who
Gave up no more than life, while you,
Already free among the dead,
Your rags stripped off, your fetters shed,
Surrendered what all other men
Irrevocably keep, and when
Your battered ship at anchor lay
Seemingly safe in the dark bay
No ripple stirs, obediently
Put out a second time to sea
Well knowing that your death (in vain
Died once) must all be died again?

## FIVE SONNETS

### I

You think that we who do not shout and shake
Our fists at God when youth or bravery die
Have colder blood or hearts less apt to ache
Than yours who rail. I know you do. Yet why?
You have what sorrow always longs to find,
Someone to blame, some enemy in chief;
Anger's the anaesthetic of the mind,
It does men good, it fumes away their grief.
We feel the stroke like you; so far our fate
Is equal. After that, for us begin
Half-hopeless labours, learning not to hate,
And then to want, and then (perhaps) to win
A high, unearthly comfort, angel's food,
That seems at first mockery to flesh and blood.

## 2

There's a repose, a safety (even a taste
Of something like revenge?) in fixed despair
Which we're forbidden. We have to rise with haste
And start to climb what seems a crazy stair.
Our consolation (for we are consoled,
So much of us, I mean, as may be left
After the dreadful process has unrolled)
For one bereavement makes us more bereft.
It asks for all we have, to the last shred;
Read Dante, who had known its best and worst –
He was bereaved and he was comforted
– No one denies it, comforted – but first
Down to the frozen centre, up the vast
Mountain of pain, from world to world, he passed.


## 3

Of this we're certain; no one who dared knock
At heaven's door for earthly comfort found
Even a door – only smooth, endless rock,
And save the echo of his cry no sound.
It's dangerous to listen; you'll begin
To fancy that those echoes (hope can play
Pitiful tricks) are answers from within;
Far better to turn, grimly sane, away.
Heaven cannot thus, Earth cannot ever, give
The thing we want. We ask what isn't there
And by our asking water and make live
That very part of love which must despair
And die and go down cold into the earth
Before there's talk of springtime and re-birth.

Pitch your demands heaven-high and they'll be met.
Ask for the Morning Star and take (thrown in)
Your earthly love. Why, yes; but how to set
One's foot on the first rung, how to begin?
The silence of one voice upon our ears
Beats like the waves; the coloured morning seems
A lying brag; the face we loved appears
Fainter each night, or ghastlier, in our dreams.
'That long way round which Dante trod was meant
For mighty saints and mystics not for me,'
So Nature cries. Yet if we once assent
To Nature's voice, we shall be like the bee
That booms against the window-pane for hours
Thinking that way to reach the laden flowers.


5

'If we could speak to her,' my doctor said,
'And told her, "Not that way! All, all in vain
You weary out your wings and bruise your head,"
Might she not answer, buzzing at the pane,
"Let queens and mystics and religious bees
Talk of such inconceivables as glass;
The blunt lay worker flies at what she sees,
Look there – ahead, ahead – the flowers, the grass!"
We catch her in a handkerchief (who knows
What rage she feels, what terror, what despair?)
And shake her out – and gaily out she goes
Where quivering flowers stand thick in summer air,
To drink their hearts. But left to her own will
She would have died upon the window-sill.'

# EVENSONG

Now that night is creeping
O'er our travail'd senses,
To Thy care unsleeping
We commit our sleep.
Nature for a season
Conquers our defences,
But th' eternal Reason
Watch and ward will keep.

All the soul we render
Back to Thee completely,
Trusting Thou wilt tend her
Through the deathlike hours,
And all night remake her
To Thy likeness sweetly,
Then with dawn awake her
And give back her powers.

Slumber's less uncertain
Brother soon will bind us
– Darker falls the curtain,
Stifling-close 'tis drawn:
But amidst that prison
Still Thy voice can find us,
And, as Thou has risen,
Raise us in Thy dawn.

# THE APOLOGIST'S EVENING PRAYER

From all my lame defeats and oh! much more
From all the victories that I seemed to score;
From cleverness shot forth on Thy behalf
At which, while angels weep, the audience laugh;
From all my proofs of Thy divinity,
Thou, who wouldst give no sign, deliver me.

Thoughts are but coins. Let me not trust, instead
Of Thee, their thin-worn image of Thy head.
From all my thoughts, even from my thoughts of
    Thee,
O thou fair Silence, fall, and set me free.
Lord of the narrow gate and the needle's eye,
Take from me all my trumpery lest I die.


# FOOTNOTE TO ALL PRAYERS

He whom I bow to only knows to whom I bow
When I attempt the ineffable Name, murmuring *Thou*,
And dream of Pheidian fancies and embrace in heart
Symbols (I know) which cannot be the thing Thou art.
Thus always, taken at their word, all prayers blaspheme
Worshipping with frail images a folk-lore dream,
And all men in their praying, self-deceived, address
The coinage of their own unquiet thoughts, unless
Thou in magnetic mercy to Thyself divert
Our arrows, aimed unskilfully, beyond desert;
And all men are idolators, crying unheard
To a deaf idol, if Thou take them at their word.

Take not, oh Lord, our literal sense. Lord, in Thy great,
Unbroken speech our limping metaphor translate.

# AFTER PRAYERS, LIE COLD

Arise my body, my small body, we have striven
Enough, and He is merciful; we are forgiven.
Arise small body, puppet-like and pale, and go,
White as the bed-clothes into bed, and cold as snow,
Undress with small, cold fingers and put out the light,
And be alone, hush'd mortal, in the sacred night,
– A meadow whipt flat with the rain, a cup
Emptied and clean, a garment washed and folded up,
Faded in colour, thinned almost to raggedness
By dirt and by the washing of that dirtiness.
Be not too quickly warm again. Lie cold; consent
To weariness' and pardon's watery element.
Drink up the bitter water, breathe the chilly death;
Soon enough comes the riot of our blood and breath.

# Part v

# A FAREWELL TO
# SHADOW-LANDS

# EPIGRAMS AND EPITAPHS

### 1

Lady, to this fair breast I know but one
Fair rival; to the heart beneath it, none.

### 2

Have you not seen that in our days
Of any whose story, song, or art
Delights us, our sincerest praise
Means, when all's said, 'You break my heart'?

### 3

I woke from a fool's dream, to find all spent
Except one little sixpence, worn and bent.
The same day, in the nick of time, I found
The market where my sixpence buys a pound.
Sirs, tell me was the bargain good or bad?
The price was cheap. The price was all I had.

### 4

Strange that a trick of light and shade could look
So like a living form that, first, I gave
The shadow mind and meaning: then, mistook
His will for mine; and, last, became his slave.

### 5

If we had remembered earlier our Father's house
Where we grew together, and that old kindness,
You would not now be dying, oh my sister, my spouse,
Pierced with my sword in the battle's heat and the blindness.

## 6

Save yourself. Run and leave me. I must go back.
Though we have escaped the sentry and are past the wall,
Though returning means mockery and the whip and the rack,
Yet their sending is too strong; I must turn at their call.
Save yourself. Leave me. I must go back.

## 7

... Spirit? Who names her lies.
Who cares for a bodiless ghost without any eyes
Or feet to run with at all, or ear for the call
Of the rushing rain, and the crack of the opening skies?
But I'd have a body, a bird's fleet body that flies.

## 8

All things (e.g. a camel's journey through
A needle's eye) are possible, it's true.
But picture how the camel feels, squeezed out
In one long bloody thread from tail to snout.

## 9

Lady, a better sculptor far
Chiselled those curves you smudge and mar,
And God did more than lipstick can
To justify your mouth to man.

## 10

Erected by her sorrowing brothers
In memory of Martha Clay.
Here lies one who lived for others;
Now she has peace. And so have they.

She was beautifully, delicately made,
So small, so unafraid,
    Till the bomb came.
    Bombs are the same,
Beautifully, delicately made.

No; the world will not break,
    Time will not stop.
Do not for the dregs mistake
    The first bitter drop.

When first the collar galls
    Tired horses know
Stable's not near. Still falls
    The whip. There's far to go.

Here lies one kind of speech
That in the unerring hour when each
Idle syllable must be
Weighed upon the balance, she,
Though puzzled and ashamed, I think,
To watch the scales of thousands sink,
Will see with her old woodland air
(That startled, yet unflinching stare,
Half elf, half squirrel, all surprise)
Here quiver and demurely rise.

From end to end of the bright airy ward,
From end to end of each delirious day,

The wireless gibbered, hammered, squealed and roared;
That was the pain no drugs could drive away.
I asked for an hour of silence – half an hour –
Ten minutes – to die sane. It wasn't granted.
Why should one Prig, one High-brow, have the power
To stop what all those honest fellows wanted?
Therefore, oh God, if heaven, as they tell,
Is full of music, yet in mercy save
For me one nook of silence even in hell,
And therefore, stranger, tip-toe past this grave;
And let posterity know this of me –
I died both for, and of, democracy.


15

(Emendation for the end of Goethe's *Faust*)
   Solids whose shadow lay
   Across time, here
   (All subterfuge dispelled)
   Show hard and clear;
   Fondled impossibles
   Wither outside;
   Within, the Wholly Masculine
   Confronts His bride.


16

My grave my pillory, by this blabbing stone
     Forbidden to sleep unknown,
I feel like fire my neighbours' eyes because
     All here know what I was.
Think, stranger, of that moment when I too
     First, and forever, knew.

Here lies the whole world after one
Peculiar mode; a buried sun,
Stars and immensities of sky
And cities here discarded lie.
The prince who owned them, having gone,
Left them as things not needed on
His journey; yet with hope that he,
Purged by aeonian poverty
In lenten lands, hereafter can
Resume the robes he wore as man.

# APPENDIX

## *Previous publications of poems already printed*

Such poems are listed below in alphabetical order, the title being followed by (1) the abbreviation 'Rev.' when the text first published has been revised by the author; (2) the abbreviation 'Or.' introducing the original title, when it differs from that given in this volume; (3) the publication, volume, date and page-number of the original issue. The following abbreviations are used for periodicals, etc.

CR   *The Cambridge Review*
M   *The Month*
OM   *The Oxford Magazine*
P   *Punch*
S   *The Spectator*
TT   *Time and Tide*
TLS   *The Times Literary Supplement*

*Pilgrim's Regress* C. S. Lewis: *The Pilgrim's Regress: An Allegorical Apology for Christianity, Reason, and Romanticism.* London: Geoffrey Bles Ltd, 1943.

## *Published Poems*

THE ADAM AT NIGHT (Rev. Or 'Adam at Night') *P.* CCXVI (May 11, 1949) p. 510.

THE ADAM UNPARADISED (Rev. Or. 'A Footnote to Pre-History'). *P*, CCXVII (Sept. 14, 1949) p. 304.

AFTER ARISTOTLE. *OM*, LXXIV (Feb. 23, 1956), p. 296.

AS ONE OLDSTER TO ANOTHER (Rev.). *P*, CCXVIII (March 15, 1950), pp. 294-5.

BALLADE OF DEAD GENTLEMEN. *P*, CCXX (March 28, 1951), p. 386.

THE BIRTH OF LANGUAGE (Rev.). *P*, CCX (Jan. 9, 1946), p. 32.

CAUGHT, *Pilgrim's Regress*, pp. 147-8.

A CLICHÉ CAME OUT OF ITS CAGE (Rev. part I) *Nine: A Magazine of Poetry and Criticism*, II (May, 1950), p. 114.

THE CONDEMNED (Rev. Or. 'Under Sentence'). *S, CLXXV* (Sept. 7, 1945), p. 219.

A CONFESSION (Rev. Or. *Spartan Nactus*). *P, CCXXVII* (Dec. 1, 1954), p. 685.

CORONATION MARCH. *OM, LV* (May 6, 1937), p. 565.

THE COUNTRY OF THE BLIND. *P, CCXXI* (Sept. 12, 1951), p. 303.

THE DAY WITH A WHITE MARK (Rev.) *P, CCXVII* (Aug. 17, 1949), p. 170.

DECEPTION. *Pilgrim's Regress*, p. 187.

DIVINE JUSTICE. *Pilgrim's Regress*, p. 180.

DONKEY'S DELIGHT (Rev.) *P, CCXIII* (Nov. 5, 1947), p. 442.

DRAGON-SLAYER. *Pilgrim's Regress*, pp. 195-6.

THE DRAGON SPEAKS (Rev.). *Pilgrim's Regress*, pp. 192-3.

EPIGRAMS AND EPITAPHS:

No. 11 (Or. 'Epitaph'). *TT, XXIII* (June 6, 1942), p. 460;

No. 12 (Or. 'On Receiving Bad News'). *TT, XXVI* (Dec. 29, 1945), p. 1093;

No. 14 (Rev. Or. 'Epitaph'). *S, CLXXXI* (July 30, 1948), p. 142;

No. 15 (Rev. Or. 'Epanorthosis (for the end of Goethe's *Faust*)'). *CR, LXXVII* (May 26, 1956), p. 610;

No. 16 (Or. 'Epitaph in a Village Churchyard'). *TT, XXX* March 19, 1949), p. 272;

No. 17 (Or 'Epitaph'). *M, II* (July, 1949), p. 8.

EVOLUTIONARY HYMN. *CR, LXXIX* (Nov. 30, 1957), p. 227.

AN EXPOSTULATION (Against too many writers of science fiction). *Magazine of Fantasy and Science Fiction*, XVI (June, 1959), p. 47.

FOOTNOTE TO ALL PRAYERS (Rev.) *Pilgrim's Regress*, pp. 144-5.

FORBIDDEN PLEASURE. *Pilgrim's Regress*, p. 189.

THE FUTURE OF FORESTRY. *OM, LVI* (Feb. 10, 1938), p. 383.

HERMIONE IN THE HOUSE OF PAULINA (Rev.) *Augury: An Oxford Miscellany of Verse and Prose*, ed. by Alex M. Hardie and Keith C. Douglas. Oxford: Basil Blackwell, 1940, p. 28.

IMPENITENCE. *P, CCXV* (July, 1953), p. 91.

THE LANDING (Rev.). *P*, CCXV (Sept. 15, 1948), p. 237.

THE LAST OF THE WINE (Rev. Or. 'The End of the Wine'). *P*, CCXIII (Dec. 3, 1947), p. 538.

THE LATE PASSENGER (Rev. Or. 'The Sailing of the Ark'). *P*, CCXV (Aug. 11, 1948), p. 124.

LEGION (Rev.). *M*, XIII (April, 1955), p. 210.

*LE ROI S'AMUSE* (Rev.). *P*, CCXIII (Oct. 1, 1947), p. 324.

LILITH. *Pilgrim's Regress*, pp. 190-1.

THE MAGICIAN AND THE DRYAD. (Rev. Or. 'Conversation Piece: The Magician and the Dryad'). *P*, CCXVII (July 20, 1949), p. 71.

'MAN IS A LUMPE WHERE ALL BEASTS KNEADED BE' (Rev. Or. 'The Shortest Way Home'), *OM*, LII (May 10, 1934), p. 665.

THE METEORITE. *TT*, XXVII (Dec. 7, 1946), p. 1183.

THE NAKED SEED. *Pilgrim's Regress*, p. 162.

NARNIAN SUITE (Rev. Part 2). *P*, CCXXV (Nov. 4, 1953), p. 553.

NEARLY THEY STOOD. *Pilgrim's Regress*, pp. 181-2.

*ODORA CANUM VIS* (A defence of certain modern biographers and critics) (Rev.). *M*, XI (May, 1954), p. 272.

ON THE ATOMIC BOMB (Metrical Experiment). *S*, CLXXV (Dec., 28, 1945), p. 619.

ON BEING HUMAN (Rev.). *P*, CCX (May 8, 1946), p. 402.

ON A PICTURE BY CHIRICO (Rev.). *S*, CLXXXII (May 6, 1949), p. 607.

ON A THEME FROM NICHOLAS OF CUSA (Rev. Or. 'On Another Theme from Nicholas of Cusa'). *TLS* (Jan. 21, 1955), p. 43.

PAN'S PURGE, *P*, CCXII (Jan. 15, 1947), p. 71.

PATTERN (Rev. Or. 'Experiment'). *S*, CLXI (Dec. 9, 1938), p. 998.

PILGRIM'S PROBLEM. *M*, VII (May, 1952), p. 275.

PINDAR SANG (Rev. Or. 'Arrangement of Pindar'). *Mandrake*, I, No. 6 (1949), pp. 43-5.

THE PLANETS. *Lysistrata*, II (May, 1935), pp. 21-4.

POSTURING. *Pilgrim's Regress*, pp. 184-5.

PRAYER (The original version). Lewis' revision of this poem is published 'anonymously' in his *Letters to Malcolm: Chiefly on Prayer* (Geoffrey Bles Ltd, 1964), pp. 92-3.

THE PRODIGALITY OF FIRDAUSI (Rev.). *P.* CCXV (Dec. 1, 1948), p. 510.

THE PRUDENT JAILER (Rev. Or. 'The Romantics'). *New English Weekly*, XXX (Jan. 16, 1947), p. 130.

THE SALAMANDER. *S*, CLXXIV (June 8, 1945), p. 521.

SCAZONS (Rev.) *Pilgrim's Regress*, p. 198.

SCHOLAR'S MELANCHOLY. *OM*, LII (May 24, 1934), p. 734.

SCIENCE-FICTION CRADLESONG (Rev. Or. 'Cradle-Song based on a Theme from Nicholas of Cusa'). *TLS* (June 11, 1954), p. 375.

SOLOMON (Rev.). *P*, CCXI (Aug. 14, 1946), p. 136.

SONNET. *OM*, LIV (May 14, 1936), p. 575.

TO CHARLES WILLIAMS (Rev. Or. 'On the Death of Charles Williams'). *Britain To-day*, No. 112 (Aug. 1945), p. 14.

TO A FRIEND (Rev. Or. 'To G.M.'). *S*, CLXIX (Oct. 9, 1942) p. 335.

TO THE AUTHOR OF 'FLOWERING RIFLE' (Rev. Or. 'To Mr. Roy Campbell'). *The Cherwell*, LVI (May 6, 1939), p. 35.

THE TRUE NATURE OF GNOMES, *P*, CCXI (Oct. 16, 1946), p. 310.

THE TURN OF THE TIDE (Rev.). *P*, (Almanac), CCXVI (Nov. 1, 1948).

TWO KINDS OF MEMORY (Rev.). *TT*, XXVIII (Aug. 7, 1947), p. 859.

VIRTUE'S INDEPENDENCE. *Pilgrim's Regress*, p. 183.

VITREA CIRCLE (Rev.). *P*, CCXIV (June 23, 1948), p. 543.

VOWELS AND SIRENS (Rev.). *TLS* (Special Autumn Issue), (Aug. 29, 1952), p. xiv

WHAT THE BIRD SAID EARLY IN THE YEAR (Rev. Or. *'Chanson d'Adventure'*). *OM*, LVI (May 19, 1938), p. 638.

WHEN THE CURTAIN'S DOWN. *Pilgrim's Regress*, p. 197.

WORMWOOD. *Pilgrim's Regress*, p. 177.

YOUNG KING COLE (Rev. Or. 'Dangerous oversight'). *P*, CCXII (May 21, 1947), p. 434.

# SPIRITS IN BONDAGE
## A CYCLE OF LYRICS

The land where I shall never be
The love that I shall never see.

# CONTENTS

# PROLOGUE

As of old Phoenician men, to the Tin Isles sailing
Straight against the sunset and the edges of the earth,
Chaunted loud above the storm and the strange sea's wailing,
Legends of their people and the land that gave them birth –
Sang aloud to Baal-Peor, sang unto the horned maiden,
Sang how they should come again with the Brethon treasure laden,
Sang of all the pride and glory of their hardy enterprise,
How they found the outer islands, where the unknown stars arise;
And the rowers down below, rowing hard as they could row,
Toiling at the stroke and feather through the wet and weary
weather,
Even they forgot their burden in the measure of a song,
And the merchants and the masters and the bondsmen all together,
Dreaming of the wondrous islands, brought the gallant ship along;

So in mighty deeps alone on the chainless breezes blown
In my coracle of verses I will sing of lands unknown,
Flying from the scarlet city where a Lord that knows no pity
Mocks the broken people praying round his iron throne,
Sing about the Hidden country fresh and full of quiet green.
Sailing over seas uncharted to a port that none has seen.

# Part 1

# THE PRISON HOUSE

## SATAN SPEAKS

I am Nature, the Mighty Mother,
I am the law: ye have none other.

I am the flower and the dewdrop fresh,
I am the lust in your itching flesh.

I am the battle's filth and strain,
I am the widow's empty  pain.

I am the sea to smother your breath,
I am the bomb, the falling death.

I am the fact and the crushing reason
To thwart your fantasy's new-born treason.

I am the spider making her net,
I am the beast with jaws blood-wet.

I am the wolf that follows the sun
And I will catch him ere day be done.

# FRENCH NOCTURNE
### (Monchy-Le-Preux)

Long leagues on either hand the trenches spread
And all is still; now even this gross line
Drinks in the frosty silences divine,
The pale, green moon is riding overhead.

The jaws of a sacked village, stark and grim,
Out on the ridge have swallowed up the sun,
And in one angry streak his blood has run
To left and right along the horizon dim.

There comes a buzzing plane: and now, it seems
Flies straight into the moon. Lo! where he steers
Across the pallid globe and surely nears
In that white land some harbour of dear dreams!

False, mocking fancy! Once I too could dream,
Who now can only see with vulgar eye
That he's no nearer to the moon than I
And she's a stone that catches the sun's beam.

What call have I to dream of anything?
I am a wolf. Back to the world again,
And speech of fellow-brutes that once were men
Our throats can bark for slaughter: cannot sing.

# THE SATYR

When the flowery hands of spring
Forth their woodland riches fling,
   Through the meadows, through the valleys
Goes the satyr carolling.

From the mountain and the moor,
Forest green and ocean shore
   All the faerie kin he rallies
Making music evermore.

See! the shaggy pelt doth grow
On his twisted shanks below,
   And his dreadful feet are cloven
Though his brow be white as snow –

Though his brow be clear and white
And beneath it fancies bright,
   Wisdom and high thoughts are woven
And the musics of delight,

Though his temples too be fair
Yet two horns are growing there
   Bursting forth to part asunder
All the riches of his hair.

Faerie maidens he may meet
Fly the horns and cloven feet,
   But, his sad brown eyes with wonder
Seeing – stay from their retreat.

## VICTORY

Roland is dead, Cuchulain's crest is low,
The battered war-gear wastes and turns to rust,
And Helen's eyes and Iseult's lips are dust
And dust the shoulders and the breasts of snow.

The faerie people from our woods are gone,
No Dryads have I found in all our trees.
No Triton blows his horn about our seas
And Arthur sleeps far hence in Avalon.

The ancient songs they wither as the grass
And waste as doth a garment waxen old,
All poets have been fools who thought to mould
A monument more durable than brass.

For these decay: but not for that decays
The yearning, high, rebellious spirit of man
That never rested yet since life began
From striving with red Nature and her ways.

Now in the filth of war, the baresark shout
Of battle, it is vexed. And yet so oft
Out of the deeps, of old, it rose aloft
That they who watch the ages may not doubt.

Though often bruised, oft broken by the rod,
Yes, like the phoenix, from each fiery bed
Higher the stricken spirit lifts its head
And higher – till the beast become a god.

# IRISH NOCTURNE

Now the grey mist comes creeping up
From the waste ocean's weedy strand
And fills the valley, as a cup
Is filled of evil drink in a wizard's hand;
And the trees fade out of sight,
Like dreary ghosts unhealthily,
Into the damp, pale night,
Till you almost think that a clearer eye could see
Some shape come up of a demon seeking apart
His meat, as Grendel sought in Harte
The thanes that sat by the wintry log –
Grendel or the shadowy mass
Of Balor, or the man with the face of clay,
The grey, grey walker who used to pass
Over the rock-arch nightly to his prey.
But here at the dumb, slow stream where the willows hang,
With never a wind to blow the mists apart,
Bitter and bitter it is for thee, O my heart,
Looking upon this land, where poets sang,
Thus with the dreary shroud
Unwholesome, over it spread,
And knowing the fog and the cloud
In her people's heart and head
Even as it lies for ever upon her coasts
Making them dim and dreamy lest her sons should ever arise
And remember all their boasts;
For I know that the colourless skies
And the blurred horizons breed
Lonely desire and many words and brooding and never a deed.

## SPOOKS

Last night I dreamed that I was come again
Unto the house where my belovèd dwells
After long years of wandering and pain.

And I stood out beneath the drenching rain
And all the street was bare, and black with night,
But in my true love's house was warmth and light.

Yet I could not draw near nor enter in,
And long I wondered if some secret sin
Or old, unhappy anger held me fast;

Till suddenly it came into my head
That I was killed long since and lying dead –
Only a homeless wraith that way had passed.

So thus I found my true love's house again
And stood unseen amid the winter night
And the lamp burned within, a rosy light,
And the wet street was shining in the rain.

# APOLOGY

If men should ask, Despoina, why I tell
Of nothing glad nor noble in my verse
To lighten hearts beneath this present curse
And build a heaven of dreams in real hell,

Go you to them and speak among them thus:
"There were no greater grief than to recall,
Down in the rotting grave where the lithe worms crawl,
Green fields above that smiled so sweet to us."

Is it good to tell old tales of Troynovant
Or praises of dead heroes, tried and sage,
Or sing the queens of unforgotten age,
Brynhild and Maeve and virgin Bradamant?

How should I sing of them? Can it be good
To think of glory now, when all is done,
And all our labour underneath the sun
Has brought us this – and not the thing we would?

All these were rosy visions of the night,
The loveliness and wisdom feigned of old.
But now we wake. The East is pale and cold,
No hope is in the dawn, and no delight.

## ODE FOR NEW YEAR'S DAY

Woe unto you, ye sons of pain that are this day in earth,
Now cry for all your torment: now curse your hour of birth
And the fathers who begat you to a portion nothing worth.
And Thou, my own belovèd, for as brave as ere thou art,
Bow down thine head, Despoina, clasp thy pale arms over it,
Lie low with fast-closed eyelids, clenched teeth, enduring heart,
For sorrow on sorrow is coming wherein all flesh has part.
The sky above is sickening, the clouds of God's hate cover it,
Body and soul shall suffer beyond all word or thought,
Till the pain and noisy terror that these first years have wrought
Seem but the soft arising and prelude of the storm
That fiercer still and heavier with sharper lightnings fraught
Shall pour red wrath upon us over a world deform.

Thrice happy, O Despoina, were the men who were alive
In the great age and the golden age when still the cycle ran
On upward curve and easily, for then both maid and man
And beast and tree and spirit in the green earth could thrive.
But now one age is ending, and God calls home the stars
And looses the wheel of the ages and sends it spinning back
Amid the death of nations, and points a downward track,
And madness is come over us and great and little wars.
He has not left one valley, one isle of fresh and green
Where old friends could forgather amid the howling wreck.
It's vainly we are praying. We cannot, cannot check
The Power who slays and puts aside the beauty that has been.

It's truth they tell, Despoina, none hears the heart's complaining
For Nature will not pity, nor the red God lend an ear.
Yet I too have been mad in the hour of bitter paining
And lifted up my voice to God, thinking that he could hear
The curse wherewith I cursed Him because the Good was dead.

But lo! I am grown wiser, knowing that our own hearts
Have made a phantom called the Good, while a few years have sped
Over a little planet. And what should the great Lord know of it.
Who tosses the dust of chaos and gives the suns their parts?
Hither and thither he moves them; for an hour we see the show of
    it;
Only a little hour, and the life of the race is done.
And here he builds a nebula, and there he slays a sun
And works his own fierce pleasure. All things he shall fulfil,
And O, my poor Despoina, do you think he ever hears
The wail of hearts he has broken, the sound of human ill?
He cares not for our virtues, our little hopes and fears,
And how could it all go on, love, if he knew of laughter and tears?

Ah, sweet, if a man could cheat him! If you could flee away
Into some other country beyond the rosy West,
To hide in the deep forests and be for ever at rest
From the rankling hate of God and the outworn world's decay!

## NIGHT

After the fret and failure of this day,
And weariness of thought, O Mother Night,
Come with soft kiss to soothe our care away
And all our little tumults set to right;
Most pitiful of all death's kindred fair,
Riding above us through the curtained air
On thy dusk car, thou scatterest to the earth
Sweet dreams and drowsy charms of tender might
And lovers' dear delight before to-morrow's birth.
Thus art thou wont thy quiet lands to leave
And pillared courts beyond the Milky Way,
Wherein thou tarriest all our solar day
While unsubstantial dreams before thee weave
A foamy dance, and fluttering fancies play
About thy palace in the silver ray
Of some far, moony globe. But when the hour,
The long-expected comes, the ivory gates
Open on noiseless hinge before thy bower
Unbidden, and the jewelled chariot waits
With magic steeds. Thou from the fronting rim
Bending to urge them, whilst thy sea-dark hair
Falls in ambrosial ripples o'er each limb,
With beautiful pale arms, untrammelled, bare
For horsemanship, to those twin chargers fleet
Dost give full rein across the fires that glow
In the wide floor of heaven, from off their feet
Scattering the powdery star-dust as they go.
Come swiftly down the sky, O Lady Night,
Fall through the shadow-country, O most kind,
Shake out thy strands of gentle dreams and light
For chains, wherewith thou still art used to bind
With tenderest love of careful leeches' art

The bruised and weary heart
In slumber blind.

X

## TO SLEEP

I will find out a place for thee, O Sleep –
A hidden wood among the hill-tops green,
Full of soft streams and little winds that creep
    The murmuring boughs between.

A hollow cup above the ocean placed
Where nothing rough, nor loud, nor harsh shall be,
But woodland light and shadow interlaced
    And summer sky and sea.

There in the fragrant twilight I will raise
A secret altar of the rich sea sod,
Whereat to offer sacrifice and praise
    Unto my lonely god:

Due sacrifice of his own drowsy flowers,
The deadening poppies in an ocean shell
Round which through all forgotten days and hours
    The great seas wove their spell.

So may he send me dreams of dear delight
And draughts of cool oblivion, quenching pain,
And sweet, half-wakeful moments in the night
    To hear the falling rain.

And when he meets me at the dusk of day
To call me home for ever, this I ask –
That he may lead me friendly on that way
    And wear no frightful mask.

[177]

# IN PRISON

I cried out for the pain of man,
I cried out for my bitter wrath
Against the hopeless life that ran
For ever in a circling path
From death to death since all began;
Till on a summer night
I lost my way in the pale starlight
And saw our planet, far and small,
Through endless depths of nothing fall
A lonely pin-prick spark of light,
Upon the wide, enfolding night,
With leagues on leagues of stars above it,
And powdered dust of stars below –
Dead things that neither hate nor love it
Nor even their own loveliness can know,
Being but cosmic dust and dead.
And if some tears be shed,
Some evil God have power,
Some crown of sorrows sit
Upon a little world for a little hour –
Who shall remember? Who shall care for it?

## *DE PROFUNDIS*

Come let us curse our Master ere we die,
For all our hopes in endless ruin lie.
The good is dead. Let us curse God most High.

Four thousand years of toil and hope and thought
Wherein men laboured upward and still wrought
New worlds and better, Thou hast made as naught.

We built us joyful cities, strong and fair,
Knowledge we sought and gathered wisdom rare.
And all this time you laughed upon our care,

And suddenly the earth grew black with wrong,
Our hope was crushed and silenced was our song,
The heaven grew loud with weeping. Thou art strong.

Come then and curse the Lord. Over the earth
Gross darkness falls, and evil was our birth
And our few happy days of little worth.

Even if it be not all a dream in vain
– The ancient hope that still will rise again –
Of a just God that cares for earthly pain,

Yet far away beyond our labouring night,
He wanders in the depths of endless light,
Singing alone his musics of delight;

Only the far, spent echo of his song,
Our dungeons and deep cells can smite along,
And Thou art nearer. Thou art very strong.

O universal strength, I know it well,
It is but froth of folly to rebel,
For thou art Lord and hast the keys of Hell.

Yet I will not bow down to thee nor love thee,
For looking in my own heart I can prove thee,
And know this frail, bruised being is above thee.

Our love, our hope, our thirsting for the right,
Our mercy and long seeking of the light,
Shall we change these for thy relentless might?

Laugh then and slay. Shatter all things of worth,
Heap torment still on torment for thy mirth –
Thou art not Lord while there are Men on earth.

## SATAN SPEAKS

I am the Lord your God: even he that made
Material things, and all these signs arrayed
Above you and have set beneath the race
Of mankind, who forget their Father's face
And even while they drink my light of day
Dream of some other gods and disobey
My warnings, and despise my holy laws,
Even tho' their sin shall slay them. For which cause,
Dreams dreamed in vain, a never-filled desire
And in close flesh a spiritual fire,
A thirst for good their kind shall not attain,
A backward cleaving to the beast again.
A loathing for the life that I have given,
A haunted, twisted soul for ever riven
Between their will and mine – such lot I give
While still in my despite the vermin live.
They hate my world! Then let that other God
Come from the outer spaces glory-shod,
And from this castle I have built on Night
Steal forth my own thought's children into light,
If such an one there be. But far away
He walks the airy fields of endless day,
And my rebellious sons have called Him long
And vainly called. My order still is strong
And like to me nor second none I know.
Whither the mammoth went this creature too shall go.

# THE WITCH

Trapped amid the woods with guile
They've led her bound in fetters vile
To death, a deadlier sorceress
Than any born for earth's distress
Since first the winner of the fleece
Bore home the Colchian witch to Greece –
Seven months with snare and gin
They've sought the maid o'erwise within
The forest's labyrinthine shade.
The lonely woodman half afraid
Far off her ragged form has seen
Sauntering down the alleys green,
Or crouched in godless prayer alone
At eve before a Druid stone.
But now the bitter chase is won,
The quarry's caught, her magic's done,
The bishop's brought her strongest spell
To naught with candle, book, and bell;
With holy water splashed upon her,
She goes to burning and dishonour
Too deeply damned to feel her shame,
For, though beneath her hair of flame
Her thoughtful head be lowly bowed
It droops for meditation proud
Impenitent, and pondering yet
Things no memory can forget,
Starry wonders she has seen
Brooding in the wildwood green
With holiness. For who can say
In what strange crew she loved to play,
What demons or what gods of old
Deep mysteries unto her have told

At dead of night in worship bent
At ruined shrines magnificent,
Or how the quivering will she sent
Alone into the great alone
Where all is loved and all is known,
Who now lifts up her maiden eyes
And looks around with soft surprise
Upon the noisy, crowded square,
The city oafs that nod and stare,
The bishop's court that gathers there,
The faggots and the blackened stake
Where sinners die for justice' sake?
Now she is set upon the pile,
The mob grows still a little while,
Till lo! before the eager folk
Up curls a thin, blue line of smoke.
'Alas!' the full-fed burghers cry,
'That evil loveliness must die!'

## DUNGEON GRATES

So piteously the lonely soul of man
Shudders before this universal plan,
So grievous is the burden and the pain,
So heavy weighs the long, material chain
From cause to cause, too merciless for hate,
The nightmare march of unrelenting fate,
I think that he must die thereof unless
Ever and again across the dreariness
There came a sudden glimpse of spirit faces,
A fragrant breath to tell of flowery places
And wider oceans, breaking on the shore
For which the hearts of men are always sore.
It lies beyond endeavour; neither prayer
Nor fasting, nor much wisdom winneth there,
Seeing how many prophets and wise men
Have sought for it and still returned again
With hope undone. But only the strange power
Of unsought Beauty in some casual hour
Can build a bridge of light or sound or form
To lead you out of all this strife and storm;
When of some beauty we are grown a part
Till from its very glory's midmost heart
Out leaps a sudden beam of larger light
Into our souls. All things are seen aright
Amid the blinding pillar of its gold,
Seven times more true than what for truth we hold
In vulgar hours. The miracle is done
And for one little moment we are one
With the eternal stream of loveliness
That flows so calm, aloof from all distress
Yet leaps and lives around us as a fire
Making us faint with overstrong desire

To sport and swim for ever in its deep –
Only a moment O! but we shall keep
Our vision still. One moment was enough,
We know we are not made of mortal stuff.
And we can bear all trials that come after,
The hate of men and the fool's loud bestial laughter
And Nature's rule and cruelties unclean,
For we have seen the Glory – we have seen.

# THE PHILOSOPHER

Who shall be our prophet then,
Chosen from all the sons of men
To lead his fellows on the way
Of hidden knowledge, delving deep
To nameless mysteries that keep
Their secret from the solar day!
Or who shall pierce with surer eye
This shifting veil of bittersweet
And find the real things that lie
Beyond this turmoil, which we greet
With such a wasted wealth of tears?
Who shall cross over for us the bridge of fears
And pass in to the country where the ancient Mothers dwell?
Is it an elder, bent and hoar
Who, where the waste Atlantic swell
On lonely beaches make its roar,
In his solitary tower
Through the long night hour by hour
Pores on old books with watery eye
When all his youth has passed him by,
And folly is schooled and love is dead
And frozen fancy laid abed,
While in his veins the gradual blood
Slackens to a marish flood?
For he rejoiceth not in the ocean's might,
Neither the sun giveth delight,
Nor the moon by night
Shall call his feet to wander in the haunted forest lawn.
He shall no more rise suddenly in the dawn
When mists are white and the dew lies pearly
Cold and cold on every meadow,
To take his joy of the season early,

The opening flower and the westward shadow,
And scarcely can he dream of laughter and love,
They lie so many leaden years behind.
Such eyes are dim and blind,
And the sad, aching head that nods above
His monstrous books can never know
The secret we would find.
But let our seer be young and kind
And fresh and beautiful of show,
And taken ere the lustyhead
And rapture of his youth be dead,
Ere the gnawing, peasant reason
School him over-deep in treason
To the ancient high estate
Of his fancy's principate,
That he may live a perfect whole,
A mask of the eternal soul,
And cross at last the shadowy bar
To where the ever-living are.

# THE OCEAN STRAND

O leave the labouring roadways of the town,
The shifting faces and the changeful hue
Of markets, and broad echoing streets that drown
The heart's own silent music. Though they too
Sing in their proper rhythm, and still delight
The friendly ear that loves warm human kind,
Yet it is good to leave them all behind,
Now when from lily dawn to purple night
Summer is queen,
Summer is queen in all the happy land.
Far, far away among the valleys green
Let us go forth and wander hand in hand
Beyond those solemn hills that we have seen
So often welcome home the falling sun
Into their cloudy peaks when day was done –
Beyond them till we find the ocean strand
And hear the great waves run,
With the waste song whose melodies I'd follow
And weary not for many a summer day,
Born of the vaulted breakers arching hollow
Before they flash and scatter into spray.
On, if we should be weary of their play
Then I would lead you further into land
Where, with their ragged walls, the stately rocks
Shut in smooth courts and paved with quiet sand
To silence dedicate. The sea-god's flocks
Have rested here, and mortal eyes have seen
By great adventure at the dead of noon
A lonely nereid drowsing half a-swoon
Buried beneath her dark and dripping locks.

## NOON

Noon! and in the garden bower
The hot air quivers o'er the grass,
The little lake is smooth as glass
And still so heavily the hour
Drags, that scarce the proudest flower
Pressed upon its burning bed
Has strength to lift a languid head:
– Rose and fainting violet
By the water's margin set
Swoon and sink as they were dead
Though their weary leaves be fed
With the foam-drops of the pool
Where it trembles dark and cool,
Wrinkled by the fountain spraying
O'er it. And the honey-bee
Hums his drowsy melody
And wanders in his course a-straying
Through the sweet and tangled glade
With his golden mead o'erladen,
Where beneath the pleasant shade
Of the darkling boughs a maiden
– Milky limb and fiery tress,
All at sweetest random laid –
Slumbers, drunken with the excess
Of the noontide's loveliness.

## MILTON READ AGAIN
### (IN SURREY)

Three golden months while summer on us stole
I have read your joyful tale another time,
Breathing more freely in that larger clime
And learning wiselier to deserve the whole.

Your Spirit, Master, has been close at hand
And guided me, still pointing treasures rare,
Thick-sown where I before saw nothing fair
And finding waters in the barren land,

Barren once thought because my eyes were dim.
Like one I am grown to whom the common field
And often-wandered copse one morning yield
New pleasures suddenly; for over him

Falls the weird spirit of unexplained delight,
New mystery in every shady place,
In every whispering tree a nameless grace,
New rapture on the windy seaward height.

So may she come to me, teaching me well
To savour all these sweets that lie to hand
In wood and lane about this pleasant land
Though it be not the land where I would dwell.

## SONNET

The stars come out; the fragrant shadows fall
About a dreaming garden still and sweet,
I hear the unseen bats above me bleat
Among the ghostly moths their hunting call,
And twinkling glow-worms all about me crawl.
Now for a chamber dim, a pillow meet
For slumbers deep as death, a faultless sheet,
Cool, white and smooth. So may I reach the hall
With poppies strewn where sleep that is so dear
With magic sponge can wipe away an hour
Or twelve and make them naught. Why not a year,
Why could a man not loiter in that bower
Until a thousand painless cycles wore,
And then – what if it held him evermore?

# THE AUTUMN MORNING

See! the pale autumn dawn
Is faint, upon the lawn
   That lies in powdered white
    Of hoar-frost dight.

And now from tree to tree
The ghostly mist we see
   Hung like a silver pall
    To hallow all.

It wreathes the burdened air
So strangely everywhere
   That I could almost fear
    This silence drear

Where no one song-bird sings
And dream that wizard things
   Mighty for hate or love
    Were close above.

White as the fog and fair
Drifting through middle air
   In magic dances dread
    Over my head.

Yet these should know me too
Lover and bondman true,
   One that has honoured well
    The mystic spell

Of earth's most solemn hours
Wherein the ancient powers

Of dryad, elf, or faun
Or leprechaun

Oft have their faces shown
To me that walked alone
    Seashore or haunted fen
    Or mountain glen.

Wherefore I will not fear
To walk the woodlands sere
    Into this autumn day
    Far, far away.

# Part II

# HESITATION

## L'APPRENTI SORCIER

Suddenly there came to me
The music of a mighty sea
That on a bare and iron shore
Thundered with a deeper roar
Than all the tides that leap and run
With us below the real sun:
Because the place was far away,
Above, beyond our homely day,
Neighbouring close the frozen clime
Where out of all the woods of time,
Amid the frightful seraphim
The fierce, cold eyes of Godhead gleam,
Revolving hate and misery
And wars and famines yet to be.
And in my dream I stood alone
Upon a shelf of weedy stone,
And saw before my shrinking eyes
The dark, enormous breakers rise,
And hover and fall with deafening thunder
Of thwarted foam that echoed under
The ledge, through many a cavern drear,
With hollow sounds of wintry fear.
And through the waters waste and grey,
Thick-strown for many a league away,
Out of the toiling sea arose
Many a face and form of those
Thin, elemental people dear
Who live beyond our heavy sphere.
And all at once from far and near,
They all held out their arms to me,
Crying in their melody,
'Leap in! Leap in, and take thy fill

Of all the cosmic good and ill,
Be as the Living ones that know
Enormous joy, enormous woe,
Pain beyond thought and fiery bliss:
For all thy study hunted this,
On wings of magic to arise,
And wash from off thy filmèd eyes
The cloud of cold mortality,
To find the real life and be
As are the children of the deep!
Be bold and dare the glorious leap,
Or to thy shame, go, slink again
Back to the narrow ways of men.'
So all these mocked me as I stood
Striving to wake because I feared the flood.


## XXIII

## ALEXANDRINES

There is a house that most of all on earth I hate.
Though I have passed through many sorrows and have been
In bloody fields, sad seas, and countries desolate,
Yet most I fear that empty house where the grasses green
Grow in the silent court the gaping flags between,
And down the moss-grown paths and terrace no man treads
Where the old, old weeds rise deep on the waste garden beds.
Like eyes of one long dead the empty windows stare
And I fear to cross the garden, I fear to linger there,
For in that house I know a little, silent room
Where Someone's always waiting, waiting in the gloom
To draw me with an evil eye, and hold me fast –
Yet thither doom will drive me and He will win at last.

## IN PRAISE OF SOLID PEOPLE

Thank God that there are solid folk
Who water flowers and roll the lawn,
And sit and sew and talk and smoke,
And snore all through the summer dawn.

Who pass untroubled nights and days
Full-fed and sleepily content,
Rejoicing in each other's praise,
Respectable and innocent.

Who feel the things that all men feel,
And think in well-worn grooves of thought,
Whose honest spirits never reel
Before man's mystery, overwrought.

Yet not unfaithful nor unkind,
With work-day virtues surely staid,
Theirs is the sane and humble mind,
And dull affections undismayed.

O happy people! I have seen
No verse yet written in your praise,
And, truth to tell, the time has been
I would have scorned your easy ways.

But now thro' weariness and strife
I learn your worthiness indeed,
The world is better for such life
As stout, suburban people lead.

Too often have I sat alone
When the wet night falls heavily,

And fretting winds around me moan,
And homeless longing vexes me.

For lore that I shall never know,
And visions none can hope to see,
Till brooding works upon me so
A childish fear steals over me.

I look around the empty room,
The clock still ticking in its place,
And all else silent as the tomb,
Till suddenly, I think, a face

Grows from the darkness just beside.
I turn, and lo! it fades away,
And soon another phantom tide
Of shifting dreams begins to play,

And dusky galleys past me sail,
Full freighted on a faerie sea;
I hear the silken merchants hail
Across the ringing waves to me

– Then suddenly, again, the room,
Familiar books about me piled,
And I alone amid the gloom,
By one more mocking dream beguiled.

And still no nearer to the Light,
And still no further from myself,
Alone and lost in clinging night
– (The clock's still ticking on the shelf).

Then do I envy solid folk
Who sit of evenings by the fire,
After their work and doze and smoke,
And are not fretted by desire.

# Part III
# THE ESCAPE

## SONG OF THE PILGRIMS

O Dwellers at the back of the North Wind,
What have we done to you? How have we sinned
Wandering the earth from Orkney unto Ind?

With many deaths our fellowship is thinned,
Our flesh is withered in the parching wind,
Wandering the earth from Orkney unto Ind.

We have no rest. We cannot turn again
Back to the world and all her fruitless pain,
Having once sought the land where ye remain.

Some say ye are not. But, ah God! we know
That somewhere, somewhere past the Northern snow
Waiting for us the red-rose gardens blow:

– The red-rose and the white-rose gardens blow
In the green Northern land to which we go,
Surely the ways are long and the years are slow.

We have forsaken all things sweet and fair,
We have found nothing worth a moment's care
Because the real flowers are blowing there.

Land of the Lotus fallen from the sun,
Land of the Lake from whence all rivers run,
Land where the hope of all our dreams is won!

Shall we not somewhere see at close of day
The green walls of that country far away,
And hear the music of her fountains play?

So long we have been wandering all this while
By many a perilous sea and drifting isle,
We scarce shall dare to look thereon and smile.

Yea, when we are drawing very near to thee,
And when at last the ivory port we see
Our hearts will faint with mere felicity:

But we shall wake again in garden bright
Of green and gold for infinite delight,
Sleeping beneath the solemn mountains white,

While from the flowery copses still unseen
Sing out the crooning birds that ne'er have been
Touched by the hand of winter frore and lean;

And ever living queens that grow not old
And poets wise in robes of faerie gold
Whisper a wild, sweet song that first was told

Ere God sat down to make the Milky Way.
And in those gardens we shall sleep and play
For ever and for ever and a day.

Ah, Dwellers at the back of the North Wind,
What have we done to you? How have we sinned,
That ye should hide beyond the Northern wind?

Land of the Lotus, fallen from the Sun,
When shall your hidden, flowery vales be won
And all the travail of our way be done?

Very far we have searched; we have even seen
The Scythian waste that bears no soft nor green,
And near the Hideous Pass our feet have been.

We have heard Syrens singing all night long
Beneath the unknown stars their lonely song
In friendless seas beyond the Pillars strong.

Nor by the dragon-daughter of Hypocras
Nor the vale of the Devil's head we have feared to pass,
Yet is our labour lost and vain, alas!

Scouring the earth from Orkney unto Ind,
Tossed on the seas and withered in the wind,
We seek and seek your land. How have we sinned?

Or is it all a folly of the wise,
Bidding us walk these ways with blinded eyes
While all around us real flowers arise?

But, by the very God, we know, we know
That somewhere still, beyond the Northern snow
Waiting for us the red-rose gardens blow.

# SONG

Faeries must be in the woods
Or the satyrs' laughing broods –
Tritons in the summer sea,
Else how could the dead things be
Half so lovely as they are?
How could wealth of star on star
Dusted o'er the frosty night
Fill thy spirit with delight
And lead thee from this care of thine
Up among the dreams divine,
Were it not that each and all
Of them that walk the heavenly hall
Is in truth a happy isle,
Where eternal meadows smile,
And golden globes of fruit are seen
Twinkling through the orchards green;
Where the Other People go
On the bright sward to and fro?
Atoms dead could never thus
Stir the human heart of us
Unless the beauty that we see
The veil of endless beauty be,
Filled full of spirits that have trod
Far hence along the heavenly sod
And seen the bright footprints of God.

# THE ASS

I woke and rose and slipt away
To the heathery hills in the morning grey.

In a field where the dew lay cold and deep
I met an ass, new-roused from sleep.

I stroked his nose and I tickled his ears,
And spoke soft words to quiet his fears.

His eyes stared into the eyes of me
And he kissed my hands of his courtesy.

'O big, brown brother out of the waste,
How do thistles for breakfast taste?

'And do you rejoice in the dawn divine
With a heart that is glad no less than mine?

'For, brother, the depth of your gentle eyes
Is strange and mystic as the skies:

'What are the thoughts that grope behind,
Down in the mist of a donkey mind?

'Can it be true, as the wise men tell,
That you are a mask of God as well,

'And, as in us, so in you no less
Speaks the eternal Loveliness,

'And words of the lips that all things know
Among the thoughts of a donkey go?

'However it be, O four-foot brother,
Fair to-day is the earth, our mother.

'God send you peace and delight thereof,
And all green meat of the waste you love,

'And guard you well from violent men
Who'd put you back in the shafts again.'

But the ass had far too wise a head
To answer one of the things I said,

So he twitched his fair ears up and down
And turned to nuzzle his shoulder brown.

## BALLADE MYSTIQUE

The big, red house is bare and lone
The stony garden waste and sere
With blight of breezes ocean blown
To pinch the wakening of the year;
My kindly friends with busy cheer
My wretchedness could plainly show.
They tell me I am lonely here –
What do they know? What do they know?

They think that while the gables moan
And casements creak in winter drear
I should be piteously alone
Without the speech of comrades dear;
And friendly for my sake they fear,
It grieves them thinking of me so
While all their happy life is near –
What do they know? What do they know?

That I have seen the Dagda's throne
In sunny lands without a tear
And found a forest all my own
To ward with magic shield and spear,
Where, through the stately towers I rear
For my desire, around me go
Immortal shapes of beauty clear:
They do not know, they do not know.

L'ENVOI

The friends I have without a peer
Beyond the western ocean's glow,
Whither the faerie galleys steer,
They do not know: how should they know?

# NIGHT

I know a little Druid wood
Where I would slumber if I could
And have the murmuring of the stream
To mingle with a midnight dream,
And have the holy hazel trees
To play above me in the breeze,
And smell the thorny eglantine;
For there the white owls all night long
In the scented gloom divine
Hear the wild, strange, tuneless song
Of faerie voices, thin and high
As the bat's unearthly cry,
And the measure of their shoon
Dancing, dancing, under the moon,
Until, amid the pale of dawn
The wandering stars begin to swoon . . .
Ah, leave the world and come away!
The windy folk are in the glade,
And men have seen their revels, laid
In secret on some flowery lawn
Underneath the beechen covers.
Kings of old, I've heard them say,
Here have found them faerie lovers
That charmed them out of life and kissed
Their lips with cold lips unafraid,
And such a spell around them made
That they have passed beyond the mist
And found the Country-under-wave . . .

Kings of old, whom none could save!

# OXFORD

It is well that there are palaces of peace
And discipline and dreaming and desire,
Lest we forget our heritage and cease
The Spirit's work – to hunger and aspire:

Lest we forget that we were born divine,
Now tangled in red battle's animal net,
Murder the work and lust the anodyne,
Pains of the beast 'gainst bestial solace set.

But this shall never be: to us remains
One city that has nothing of the beast,
That was not built for gross, material gains,
Sharp, wolfish power or empire's glutted feast.

We are not wholly brute. To us remains
A clean, sweet city lulled by ancient streams,
A place of vision and of loosening chains,
A refuge of the elect, a tower of dreams.

She was not builded out of common stone
But out of all men's yearning and all prayer
That she might live, eternally our own,
The Spirit's stronghold – barred against despair.

## HYMN (FOR BOYS' VOICES)

All the things magicians do
Could be done by me and you
Freely, if we only knew.

Human children every day
Could play at games the faeries play
If they were but shown the way.

Every man a God would be
Laughing through eternity
If as God's his eye could see.

All the wizardries of God –
Slaying matter with a nod,
Charming spirits with his rod,

With the singing of his voice
Making lonely lands rejoice,
Leaving us no will nor choice,

Drawing headlong me and you
As the piping Orpheus drew
Man and beast the mountains through,

By the sweetness of his horn
Calling us from lands forlorn
Nearer to the widening morn –

All that loveliness of power
Could be man's peculiar dower,
Even mine, this very hour;

We should reach the Hidden Land
And grow immortal out of hand,
If we could but understand!

We could revel day and night
In all power and all delight
If we learned to think aright.

## XXXII

### 'OUR DAILY BREAD'

We need no barbarous words nor solemn spell
To raise the unknown. It lies before our feet;
There have been men who sank down into Hell
        In some suburban street,

And some there are that in their daily walks
Have met archangels fresh from sight of God,
Or watched how in their beans and cabbage-stalks
        Long files of faerie trod.

Often me too the Living voices call
In many a vulgar and habitual place,
I catch a sight of lands beyond the wall,
        I see a strange god's face.

And some day this will work upon me so
I shall arise and leave both friends and home
And over many lands a pilgrim go
        Through alien woods and foam,

Seeking the last steep edges of the earth
Whence I may leap into that gulf of light
Wherein, before my narrowing Self had birth,
        Part of me lived aright.

## HOW HE SAW ANGUS THE GOD

I heard the swallow sing in the eaves and rose
All in a strange delight while others slept,
And down the creaking stair, alone, tip-toes,
    So carefully I crept.

The house was dark with silly blinds yet drawn,
But outside the clean air was filled with light,
And underneath my feet the cold, wet lawn
    With dew was twinkling bright.

The cobwebs hung from every branch and spray
Gleaming with pearly strands of laden thread,
And long and still the morning shadows lay
    Across the meadows spread.

At that pure hour when yet no sound of man,
Stirs in the whiteness of the wakening earth,
Alone through innocent solitudes I ran
    Singing aloud for mirth.

Till I had found the open mountain heath
Yellow with gorse, and rested there and stood
To gaze upon the misty sea beneath,
    Or on the neighbouring wood,

– That little wood of hazel and tall pine
And youngling fir, where oft we have loved to see
The level beams of early morning shine
    Freshly from tree to tree.

Though in the denser wood there's many a pool
Of deep and night-born shadow lingers yet

Where the new-wakened flowers are damp and cool
    And the long grass is wet.

In the sweet heather long I rested there
Looking upon the dappled, early sky,
When suddenly, from out the shining air
    A god came flashing by.

Swift, naked, eager, pitilessly fair,
With a live crown of birds about his head,
Singing and fluttering, and his fiery hair,
    Far out behind him spread,

Streamed like a rippling torch upon the breeze
Of his own glorious swiftness: in the grass
He bruised no feathery stalk, and through the trees
    I saw his whiteness pass.

But, when I followed him beyond the wood,
Lo! he was changed into a solemn bull
That there upon the open pasture stood
    And browsed his lazy full.

## THE ROADS

I stand on the windy uplands among the hills of Down
With all the world spread out beneath, meadow and sea and town,
And ploughlands on the far-off hills that glow with friendly brown.

And ever across the rolling land to the far horizon line,
Where the blue hills border the misty west, I see the white roads
twine,
The rare roads and the fair roads that call this heart of mine.

I see them dip in the valleys and vanish and rise and bend
From shadowy dell to windswept fell, and still to the West they
wend,
And over the cold blue ridge at last to the great world's uttermost
end.

And the call of the roads is upon me, a desire in my spirit has grown
To wander forth in the highways, 'twixt earth and sky alone,
And seek for the lands no foot has trod and the seas no sail has
known:

– For the lands to the west of the evening and east of the morning's
birth,
Where the gods unseen in their valleys green are glad at the ends of
earth
And fear no morrow to bring them sorrow, nor night to quench
their mirth.

## HESPERUS

Through the starry hollow
Of the summer night
I would follow, follow
Hesperus the bright,
To seek beyond the western wave
His garden of delight.

Hesperus the fairest
Of all gods that are,
Peace and dreams thou bearest
In thy shadowy car,
And often in my evening walks
I've blessed thee from afar.

Stars without a number,
Dust the noon of night,
Thou the early slumber
And the still delight
Of the gentle twilit hours
Rulest in thy right.

When the pale skies shiver,
Seeing night is done,
Past the ocean-river,
Lightly thou dost run,
To look for pleasant, sleepy lands,
That never fear the sun.

Where, beyond the waters
Of the outer sea,
Thy triple crown of daughters
That guards the golden tree

Sing out across the lonely tide
A welcome home to thee.

And while the old, old dragon
For joy lifts up his head,
They bring thee forth a flagon
Of nectar foaming red,
And underneath the drowsy trees
Of poppies strew thy bed.

Ah! that I could follow
In thy footsteps bright,
Through the starry hollow
Of the summer night,
Sloping down the western ways
To find my heart's delight!

## THE STAR BATH

A place uplifted towards the midnight sky
Far, far away among the mountains old,
A treeless waste of rocks and freezing cold,
Where the dead, cheerless moon rode neighbouring by –
And in the midst a silent tarn there lay,
A narrow pool, cold as the tide that flows
Where monstrous bergs beyond Varanger stray,
Rising from sunless depths that no man knows;
Thither as clustering fireflies have I seen
At fixèd seasons all the stars come down
To wash in that cold wave their brightness clean
And win the special fire wherewith they crown
The wintry heavens in frost. Even as a flock
Of falling birds, down to the pool they came.
I saw them and I heard the icy shock
Of stars engulfed with hissing of faint flame
– Ages ago before the birth of men
Or earliest beast. Yet I was still the same
That now remember, knowing not where or when.

## XXXVII

### *TU NE QUÆSIERIS*

For all the lore of Lodge and Myers
I cannot heal my torn desires,
Nor hope for all that man can speer
To make the riddling earth grow clear.
Though it were sure and proven well
That I shall prosper, as they tell,
In fields beneath a different sun
By shores where other oceans run,
When this live body that was I
Lies hidden from the cheerful sky,
Yet what were endless lives to me
If still my narrow self I be
And hope and fail and struggle still,
And break my will against God's will,
To play for stakes of pleasure and pain
And hope and fail and hope again,
Deluded, thwarted, striving elf
That through the window of my self
As through a dark glass scarce can see
A warped and masked reality?
But when this searching thought of mine
Is mingled in the large Divine,
And laughter that was in my mouth
Runs through the breezes of the South,
When glory I have built in dreams
Along some fiery sunset gleams,
And my dead sin and foolishness
Grow one with Nature's whole distress,
To perfect being I shall win,
And where I end will Life begin.

# LULLABY

Lullaby! Lullaby!
There's a tower strong and high
Built of oak and brick and stone,
Stands before a wood alone.

The doors are of the oak so brown
As any ale in Oxford town,
The walls are builded warm and thick
Of the old red Roman brick,
The good grey stone is over all
In arch and floor of the tower tall.

And maidens three are living there
All in the upper chamber fair,
Hung with silver, hung with pall,
And stories painted on the wall.

And softly goes the whirring loom
In my ladies' upper room,
For they shall spin both night and day
Until the stars do pass away.

But every night at evèning
The window open wide they fling,
And one of them says a word they know
And out as three white swans they go,
And the murmuring of the woods is drowned
In the soft wings' whirring sound,
As they go flying round, around,
Singing in swans' voices high
A lonely, lovely lullaby.

## WORLD'S DESIRE

Love, there is a castle built in a country desolate,
On a rock above a forest where the trees are grim and great,
Blasted with the lightning sharp – giant builders strewn between,
And the mountains rise above, and the cold ravine
Echoes to the crushing roar and thunder of a mighty river
Raging down a cataract. Very tower and forest quiver
And the grey wolves are afraid and the call of birds is drowned,
And the thought and speech of man in the boiling water's sound.
But upon the further side of the barren, sharp ravine
With the sunlight on its turrets is the castle seen,
Calm and very wonderful, white above the green
Of the wet and waving forest, slanted all away,
Because the driving Northern wind will not rest by night or day.
Yet the towers are sure above, very might is the stead,
The gates are made of ivory, the roofs of copper red.

Round and round the warders grave walk upon the walls for ever
And the wakeful dragons couch in the ports of ivory,
Nothing is can trouble it, hate of the gods nor man's endeavour,
And it shall be a resting-place, dear heart, for you and me.

Through the wet and waving forest with an age-old sorrow laden
Singing of the world's regret wanders wild the faerie maiden,
Through the thistle and the brier, through the tangles of the thorn,
Till her eyes be dim with weeping and her homeless feet are torn.
Often to the castle gate up she looks with vain endeavour,
For her soulless loveliness to the castle winneth never.

But within the sacred court, hidden high upon the mountain,
Wandering in the castle gardens lovely folk enough there be,
Breathing in another air, drinking of a purer fountain
And among that folk, beloved, there's a place for you and me.

# DEATH IN BATTLE

Open the gates for me,
Open the gates of the peaceful castle, rosy in the West,
In the sweet dim Isle of Apples over the wide seas breast,
Open the gates for me!

Sorely pressed have I been
And driven and hurt beyond bearing this summer day,
But the heat and the pain together suddenly fall away,
All's cool and green.

But a moment agone,
Among men cursing in fight and toiling, blinded I fought,
But the labour passed on a sudden even as a passing thought,
And now – alone!

Ah, to be ever alone,
In flowery valleys among the mountains and silent wastes untrod,
In the dewy upland places, in the garden of God,
This would atone!

I shall not see
The brutal, crowded faces around me, that in their toil have grown
Into the faces of devils – yea, even as my own –
When I find thee,

O Country of Dreams!
Beyond the tide of the ocean, hidden and sunk away,
Out of the sound of battles, near to the end of day,
Full of dim woods and streams.

# A MISCELLANY OF
# ADDITIONAL POEMS

# CONTENTS

# THE HILLS OF DOWN
### (Easter 1915)

I will abide
    And make my dwelling here
Whatso betide,
    Since there is more to fear
  Out yonder. Though
    This world is drear and wan,
I dare not go
    To dreaming Avalon,
Nor look what lands
    May lie beyond the last
Strange sunset strands
    That gleam when day is past
I' the yearning west,
    Nor seek some faery town
Nor cloud land, lest
    I lose the hills of Down,
    The long, low hills of Down.

Not I alone,
    If I were gone, must weep;
Themselves would moan
    From glen to topmost steep.
Cold, snow pure wells
    Sweet with the spring tide's scent,
Forsaken fells
    That only I frequent –
And uplands bare
    Would call for me above,
Were I not there
    To roam the hills I love.
For I alone

Have loved their loneliness;
None else hath known
    Nor seen the goodliness
Of the green hills of Down.
The soft low hills of Down.

# AGAINST POTPOURRI
## *(Summer 1915)*

I saw one garner in a bowl to keep
The drowsy leaves that mid-June roses weep,
Weep for the passing of the glad young year –
And musing gazed upon the crumpled heap,
And told half dreaming every fragrant tear.


These were no worser weeds than those they say
Sad Proserpine was culling on that day
When, plucking such to deck her maiden bower,
Herself by swarthy Dis was borne away –
A harsher hand to pluck a fairer flower.


Methought: the phantom of each broken bloom,
Midst fellow ghosts, throughout the winter's gloom,
Here in this bowl, upon some carven shelf,
They'll set to breathe across a firelit room
Some lingering magic of its summer self.


They ween, it may be, in these leaves to bind
Some remnant of dead summers left behind
For a memorial. Folly! Though they shed
Some fragrance yet, there is no man shall find –
Delight and beauty here among the dead.


There lurks among these wraiths no magic scent
To conjure back to earth old seasons spent:
These tidings only shall they yield at last
That where the leaves ye did not gather went,
Their full blown summer beauty too hath passed.

Why do ye garner then the leaves that fall?
They should be left to weave the dead year's pall
And dance upon the Autumn's frosty breath.
For but one flower shall outline them all –
The eternal poppy, deathless weed of death.

# A PRELUDE
*(Summer 1915)*

When casements creak and night winds shriek
And window panes are patterned o'er
With many a fair fantastic freak
Of felon Frost, and while the door
Is rattling restless on its hinge
And cheerful fires leap up amain
The chamber roof with flame to tinge –
I turn me on my bed again.

And then once more forgotten lore
And ancient stories old in time
And goodly names long covered o'er
With slumbering ages' crusted rime
And worthy lays that did beguile
The kings of eld, dance through my brain
To stately measures strange, the while
I turn me on my bed again.

Full plain by night each faery wight
Before my drowsy eyes I see,
And sorcerer, and lady white
And churl or clown of low degree,
While dusky gallies past me sail
Full freighted on a faery main,
And silken merchants bid me hail
That turn me on my bed again.

And there I wis were nought amiss
Were I content with faery lore
To con, and faery lips to kiss
And faery songs to murmur o'er,

But I must moil and labour long
With tongue untought and careful pain
To beat my fancies into song,
And toss upon my bed again.

By midnight chimes in winter times
When tempests shook and shivered near
Upon my bed I wrought these rhymes –
Ill-done mayhap, and held too dear:
But foolish dreams will not be still,
Till one last dream hold longer reign,
Nor cease their silly songs, until
We turn to longer rest again.

## BALLADE OF A
## WINTER'S MORNING
### *(Christmas 1915)*

The rain is pattering on the leads,
The wasted garden wan and bare,
Is flooded o'er its flowerless beds;
So think no more to wander there
But rather, by this cheerful glare
Draw up beside me, friend by friend
A snugly cushioned easy chair –
A merry morning we shall spend.

And though the rain be on the leads
And far-off hills a mantle wear
Of drifting mist about their heads,
Though out to sea the sirens blare
Where ships like pallid phantoms fare
And through the steaming fog banks wend

A chilly way, we'll laugh at care
And make us merry friend by friend.

The rain is pattering on the leads,
But we this crackling blaze will share
And take fit books for drowsy heads
To bend above an easy chair –
Old tomes full oft re-read with care,
Where hoary rhymes and legends blend
With noble pictures rich and rare
To make us merry friend by friend.

And while the rain is on the leads
What song-craft sweet shall be our fare?
– The tale where Spenser's magic sheds
A slumbrous sweetness on the air
Of charmed lands, and Horace fair,
And Malory who told the end
Of Arthur, and the trumpet blare
Of him who sang Patroklos' friend.

The rain will cease upon the leads
All soon enough, the garden bare
Will blossom in those flowerless beds
When Spring returns with kindly care:
The years shall wax and wither there
Till other feet about it wend
And other lips shall call it fair
Than thine or mine, oh friend, my friend.

### l'envoi

So while the wind-foot seasons wear
Be glad, and when towards the end
Adown the dusky ways we fare,
We'll tread them bravely, friend by friend!

# LAUS MORTIS
### (Easter 1916)

Past the surge and solemn sound of ocean,
Where his river like a dragon curled
Rolls forever with untroubled motion
Round the lost, lone beaches of the world,

Near the full toned tide a cloudy glade is
Where the wandering sunbeam ever rests;
'Tis the wone of old horse-mastering Hades –
Lord of many thralls and many guests.

Only through the silvery birches quiver
Pallid lights more faint than marish-fires,
Where the soft, wan wraiths to Lethe river
Throng to quench their sorrows and desires.

Shadowy hunters there may hunt for shadows
Driving boar and deer through brake and fell,
Phantom lovers greet in darkling meadows
On the cold dew-sprinkled asphodel.

Time this people knoweth not, nor treason
Of his guile that steals swift joys away,
Nor this garish pomp of changing season
And the interflow of night and day.

These are free alike from joy and sorrow
Love and hate and thoughts that laugh and weep
Dreams may not affright, nor conquering morrow
Break the undawning twilight of their sleep.

Sad these hither beaches, where the shingle
Slowly sinks in weed and whispering sedge
Where sea birds and saddened waters mingle
Songs of sighing at the cold sea's edge.

Cut thy shallop from the shores asunder
Child of man, and drift towards the West
Where the pale lights gleam, and drifting wonder
Why so long thou tarriedst from thy rest.


## SONNET – TO SIR PHILIP SYDNEY
### *(Autumn 1916)*

Oh stainless knight of God, oh fresh young flower
Of manhood pure and faultless chivalry,
Before thy memory still we bow the knee
And turn towards thee in this darkened hour,
Who did not dream in any rose-sweet bower
Sequestered, all thy days, but even as we
Did battle in the self same troublous sea
And loved the terrible voices of its power;
For though in shepheard tale and amorous song
We hear the silver chimes of old romance,
Yet not the less the singer's arm was strong
To break in real lists no fabled lance,
Treading a nobler path than Milton trod,
To justify the ways of man to God.

## OF SHIPS
### *(Christmas 1916)*

Although they tell us that the days are fled
Wherein men loved the labour that they wrought
And fashioned answering beauties to the thought
Before the maker's joy was wholly dead,

I think that we have still a happy toil,
Albeit in one craft only, to us left,
One that a burdened age has not yet reft
Nor all our golden tyranny can spoil.

On a boat's deck this morning was I borne
Dead slow between the Twins. And there I heard,
More tunable than song of any bird,
A thousand hammers ringing in the morn.

A thousand hammers ringing all for joy
Because the soul of a ship is still the same
As when among his father's shiprights came,
To watch the work, Odysseus, then a boy.

He loved to see the master galley grow
And felt perhaps, in dreams, the spicy breeze
Of lotus-isles, and thought on endless seas
And nearest down to the ocean river flow.

And so today, be it a liner tall,
Black collier, or some galleon of old Spain,
Or some old, battered tramp, all seamed with pain,
The man of honest heart shall love them all.

'Argo' or 'Golden Hind' or 'Mary Lee',
From every country where man's foot has trod,
Sure they're all ships to brave the winds of God
And have their business in his glorious sea.

# COUPLETS
### *(Christmas 1916)*

Oh friend, the spring is mad today; the trees
Like wintry waves are tossing in the breeze
With rushing music round us and above.
The sun is bright on those green hills we love
Where now the fresh wind revels and makes mirth
O'er heathery wastes and comfortable earth
But newly cloven, rich and kind and brown.
There hidden far from this grey, careful town
And lifted high towards the rapid clouds
We'll see beneath us these unwholesome shrouds
Of hanging mist, these wreaths of dreary smoke,
And all this turmoil of the enthralled folk
Who labour. In that place, full well I know
That many an ambling journey we can go;
I know the little copses newly dressed
In baby-green – time out of mind possessed
By fairy men who nightly habit there
And through long years have made their dwelling fair
With happy toil: near by the earthy gods
Have left their cloven print in the dewy sods
That we may mark with wonder and chaste dread
At hour of noon, when, with our limbs outspread,
Lazily, in the whispering grass we lie
To gaze our full upon the windy sky
Far, far away, and kindly, friend with friend
To talk the old, old talk that has no end,
Roaming without an aim, without a chart
The unknown garden of another's heart.

I think, if it be truth, as some have taught
That these frail seeds of being are not caught
And blown upon the cosmic winds in vain
After our death, but bound in one again
Somewhere, we know not how, they live and thrive
Forever, and the proud gods will not give
The comfortable doom of quiet sleep,
Then doubt not but that from the starry deep
And utmost spaces lit by suns unknown
We should return again whence we were flown,
Leaving the bauble of a sainted crown
To walk and talk upon the hills of Down.

## CIRCE – A FRAGMENT
### *(April 1917)*

Her couch was of the mighty sea beast's tusk
With gold and Tyrian scarlet overlaid
Set in a chamber where the wafted musk
With scent of pines a wanton medly made
Through the wide pillared arches of her hall.
And these the echoing cool and peaceful shade
Of pallid marble vault and floor and wall
Hung like a tender dream about her palace all.

Without, the unbeclouded afternoon
Of an eternal summer drenched with light
Her drifting island, ready half to swoon
Beneath such heavy burden of delight:
The drunken bees forgot their toilsome flight
To slumber in the countless, drooping flowers,
And in the wide blue sea no foamcap white
Was seen, save where it wore the leaden hours
Booming about the rock and faint green Nereid bowers.

# EXERCISE
### (April 1917)

Where are the magic swords
That elves of long ago
Smithied beneath the snow
For heroes' rich rewards?

Where are the crowns of gold
That kings for worship wore,
And the banners that they bore
In the battle edge of old?

Where are the chargers true
That bore them in their day,
Bayard and Gringolet
And cloudy Sleipnr too?

Where are the speaking birds
That warned and taught our sires?
Where are the dead desires,
And long forgotten words,

The loves, the wisdoms high
The sorrows, where are they?
They are nothing at all today,
They are less than you and I.

# JOY
### (1924)

Today was all unlike another day.
The long waves of my sleep near morning broke
On happier beaches, tumbling lighted spray
Of soft dreams filled with promise. As I woke,
Like a huge bird, Joy with the feathery stroke
Of strange wings brushed me over. Sweeter air
Came never from dawn's heart. The misty smoke
Cooled it upon the hills. It touched the lair
Of each wild thing and woke the wet flowers everywhere.

I looked from the eastward window. In my thought
I boasted that this mood could never die,
'Here the new life begins. My quarry is caught.
Here is my kingdom won, and here am I.'
Shape after shape the fleeted clouds swam by,
Snow-pinnacled or flushed with early red.
The standing pools, new married to the sky,
Shone on the moors. All earth, before me spread,
Called to my feet to wander whither the wind led.

A crooked land of ever-changing lines
And mountain labyrinths hard to understand,
A land of sudden gorse and slanted pines
And far withdrawn blue valleys – a clean land
Washed with the rains, decked with the flowery hand
Of northern spring, cooled with the streams that wind
Through moss and primrose down to the sea sand.
Like Christian when his burden dropt behind,
I was set free. Pure colour purified my mind.

We do not know the language Beauty speaks,
She has no answer to our questioning,
And ease to pain and truth to one who seeks
I know she never brought and cannot bring.
But, if she wakes a moment, we must fling
Doubt at her feet, not answered, yet allayed.
She beats down wisdom suddenly. We cling
Fast to her flying skirts and she will fade,
Even at the kiss of welcome, into deepest shade.

We have no gift but tears for sacrifice.
She will not stay. But those were bitterer tears
If time's recording measure could suffice
To count the endless flash when she appears.
It is not to be weighed with empty years
And hours – they are consumed in that swift birth.
And I – I had forgotten the dull fears,
The waiting and the days that have no worth
When I returned, alone, through a grey evening earth.

And then I knew that this was all gone over.
I shall not live like this another day.
To-morrow I'll go wandering, a poor lover
Of earth, rejected, outcast every way,
And see not, hear not. Rapture will not stay
Longer than this, lest mortals grow divine
And old laws change too much. The sensitive ray
Of Beauty, her creative vision fine,
Pass. I am hers, but she will not again be mind.

# LEAVING FOR EVER
## THE HOME OF ONE'S YOUTH
### (1930)

You, beneath scraping branches, to the gate,
At evening, outward bound, have driven the last
Time of all times; the old, disconsolate
Familiar pang you have felt as in the past.

Drive on and look not out. Though from each tree
Grey memories drop and dreams thick-dusted lie
Beneath; though every other place must be
Raw, new, colonial country till we die;

Yet look not out. Think rather, 'When from France
And those old German wars we came back here,
Already it was the mind's swift, haunting glance
Towards the further past made that time dear.'

Then to that further past, still up the stream
Ascend, and think of some divine first day
In holidays from school. Even there the gleam
Of earlier memory like enchantment lay.

Always from further back breathes the thin scent,
As of cold Eden wakenings on wet lawns;
And eldest hours had elder to lament
And dreamed of irrecoverable dawns.

No more's lost now than that whose loss made bright
Old things with older things' long-lingering breath.
The past you mourn for, when it was in flight,
Lived, like the present, in continual death.

# AWAKE, MY LUTE!
## (1943)

I stood in the gloom of a spacious room
　　Where I listened for hours (on and off)
To a terrible bore with a beard like a snore
　　And a heavy rectangular cough,
Who discoursed on the habits of orchids and rabbits
　　And how an electron behaves
And a way to cure croup with solidified soup
　　In a pattern of circular waves;
Till I suddenly spied that what stood at his side
　　Was a richly upholstered baboon
With paws like the puns in a poem of Donne's
　　And a tail like a voyage to the Moon.
Then I whispered, 'Look out! For I very much doubt
　　If your colleague is really a man.'
But the lecturer said, without turning his head,
　　'Oh, that's only the Beverage Plan!'
As one might have foreseen, the whole sky became green
　　At this most injudicious remark,
For the Flood had begun and we both had to run
　　For our place in the queue to the Ark.
Then, I hardly know how (we were swimming by now),
　　The sea got all covered with scum
Made of publishers's blurbs and irregular verbs
　　Of the kind which have datives in –*um*;
And the waves were so high that far up in the sky
　　We saw the grand lobster, and heard
How he snorted, 'Compare the achievements of Blair
　　With the grave of King Alfred the Third,
And add a brief note and if possible quote,
　　And distinguish and trace and discuss
The probable course of a Methodist horse
　　When it's catching a decimal buss.'

My answer was Yes. But they marked it N.S.,*
    And a truffle-fish grabbed at my toe,
And dragged me deep down to a bombulous town
    Where the traffic was silent and slow.
Then a voice out of heaven observed, 'Quarter past seven!'
    And I threw all the waves off my head,
For that voice beyond doubt was the voice of my scout,†
    And the bed of that sea was my bed.

---

* N.S. stands for *Non Satis* (not enough), the mark given by Oxford
examiners to a question on which the candidate has failed.
† A 'scout' is a college servant.

# ESSENCE
### (1940)

Thoughts that go through my mind,
    I dare not tell them;
The alphabet of kind
    Lacks script to spell them.

Yet I remain. My will
    Some things yet can;
Thought is still one, and still
    I am called a man.

Oh of what kind, how far
    Past fire's degree
Of pureness, past a star
    In constancy;

Than light, which can possess
    Its own outgoing,
How much more one, much less
    Division knowing,

That essence must have been
    Which still I call
My self, since – thus unclean –
    It dies not all.

# CONSOLATION
## (c. 1945)

Though beer is worse and dearer
And milk has got the blues,
Though cash is short and rations
Much shorter than the queues,
Though regular as strikes and crimes,
Each day before our eyes
As a sop to the Co-Optopus
Some little business dies;

Yet sing like mad that England
is back to peacetime ways;
Not butter, eggs, or mutton,
Freedom or spacious days.
All those were non-essentials,
I've found a surer test –
If we thus caress the Muscovite,
England has turned to rest.

To ease my doubts Appeasement
Returns. Peace must be here!
The tune of glorious Munich
Once more salutes my ear;
An ancient British melody –
We heard it first begin
At the court of shifty Vortigern
Who let the Heathen in.

# FINCHLEY AVENUE
## *(c. 1950)*

We're proud of Finchley Avenue; it's quiet there,
High up and residential and in wholesome air,
With views out over London, and both straight and wide,
Shaded with copper beeches upon either side
Growing in grass, and corporation seats between.
There, as you walk, the houses can be hardly seen;
Such living walls of laurel and of privet stand,
Or sometimes rhododendron, upon either hand,
And once a wooden paling; and, above all these,
The amateurs and idlers of the world of trees –
Acacia and laburnum or such coloured things
As buzz and trill with birdsong and with insect wings.
Or else there may be banks of grass that steeply climb
Up to the hedge – reminders of the vanished time
When between fields this roadway ran of old the same
Straight course, and farmers called it by some different name.

Even at the wooden gates if you look in you see
But little, for the drives are twisted cunningly.
A gravelled sweep, a shrubbery, a slope of grass,
A gable-end, is all they show you as you pass.
But you and I are privileged and, if we please,
May enter. We were cradled in such homes as these.
Dating from nineteen-hundred or from nineteen-six,
They are are steep-roofed, unstuccoed, and reveal their bricks;
By now they are out of fashion, and their very shape
And Tuddorish graces damned with the black word Escape;
The bird-bath and the rockery and the garden seat
Scorned as a craven bourgeoisie's unearned retreat,
Whose privacy confesses a dim sense of guilt;
But all that looked so different when they were built!
These are your true antiquities. That garden lawn

Is the primordial fountain out of which was drawn
All you have since imagined of the lawn where stood
Eve's apple tree, or of the lands before the flood.
That little clump of trees (for it looks little now)
Is your original forest and has taught you how
To think of the great wilderness where trees go on
For ever after trees up the wild Amazon.
In that suburban attic with its gurgling sound
Of water pipes, in such a quiet house, you found
In early days the relics of still earlier days,
Forgotten trumpery worn to act forgotten plays,
Old books, then first remembered, calling up the past
Which then, as now, was infinitely sweet and vast.
There first you felt the wonder of deep time, the joy
And dread of Schliemann standing on the grave of Troy.

    The Avenue is full of life from nine till ten;
The owners of these houses are all hurrying then
To catch their trains. They catch them, and when these are gone,
By ones and twos the tradesmen in their vans come on;
The bread-man and the butcher and the man from Gee's
Who brings you soap and Rinso and a pound of cheese.
But even these come rarely after twelve, and soon
We sink to the dead silence of the afternoon.

    No countryside can offer so much solitude.
I have known the world less lonely in a winter wood,
For there you hear the striking of a village clock
Each hour, or the faint crowing of a distant cock.
But here is nothing. Nobody goes past. No feet
But mine. I doubt if anyone has used this seat,
Here in the shade, save only me. And here I sit
And drink the unbroken silence and reflect on it.

    What do they do? Their families have all gone hence,
Grown up. The whole long avenue exhales the sense
Of absent husbands, housework done, uncharted hours ...
Is it painful emptiness that dully lowers
Over unhappy women – or a blessed state

Of truancy wherein they darkly celebrate
Rites of some *Bona Dea* which no man may see?
I am sure they are all virtuous, yet it seems to me
Almost an eerie rashness to possess a wife
And house that go on living with their different life,
For ever inaccessible to us, all day;
For, as we knew in childhood, if the fathers stay
At home by chance, that whole day takes a different tone,
Better, or worse, it may be; but unlike its own.

## EPITAPH FOR
## HELEN JOY DAVIDMAN
### *(Summer 1963)*

Remember
Helen Joy
Davidman
D. July 1960
Loved wife of C. S. Lewis

Here the whole world (stars, water, air,
And field, and forest, as they were
Reflected in a single mind)
Like cast off clothes was left behind
In ashes yet with hope that she,
Re-born from holy poverty,
In lenten lands, hereafter may
Resume them on her Easter Day.

# INDEX OF POEMS

# INDEX OF FIRST LINES